The Ultimate Boston Red Sox Baseball Challenge

The Ultimate Boston Red Sox Baseball Challenge

David Nemec

and

Scott Flatow

Taylor Trade Publishing

Lanham • New York • Boulder • Toronto • Plymouth, UK

Published by Taylor Trade Publishing
An imprint of The Rowman & Littlefield Publishing Group, Inc.
4501 Forbes Boulevard, Suite 200, Lanham, Maryland 20706
www.rlpgtrade.com

Distributed by NATIONAL BOOK NETWORK

Library of Congress Cataloging-in-Publication Data

Nemec, David.
The ultimate Boston Red Sox baseball challenge / David Nemec and Scott Flatow.
p. cm.
ISBN-13: 978-1-58979-375-0 (pbk. : alk. paper)
ISBN-10: 1-58979-375-7 (pbk. : alk. paper)
1. Boston Red Sox (Baseball team)—Miscellanea. I. Flatow, Scott, 1966– II. Title.

GV875.B62N46 2008
796.357'640974461—dc22 2007041426

™ The paper used in this publication meets the minimum requirements of American National Standard for Information Sciences—Permanence of Paper for Printed Library Materials, ANSI/NISO Z39.48-1992.

Manufactured in the United States of America.

CONTENTS

GAME 4

GAME 5

GAME 6

Game 7

ACKNOWLEDGMENTS

The authors would like to thank Dave Zeman, Dick Thompson, and Al Blumkin for their help in fact-checking this book and offer special thanks and appreciation to Cliff Blau for providing a fourth pair of fact-checking eyes that would do even an eagle proud.

FOREWORD

I am honored to write the foreword for this groundbreaking series of baseball quiz books by Scott Flatow and David Nemec. I first encountered Scott at the Society for American Baseball Research (SABR) New York City regional meeting in 1985. He wrote an especially challenging and compelling baseball quiz for the event, which I consider myself very fortunate to have won. We became close friends soon after that meeting. Scott quickly went on to bigger and better things as both a baseball trivia player and an author. In recent years he has won three SABR National Trivia championships (two team and one individual). Scott's 1995 team set the current SABR team record for the widest margin of victory, and he later posted the highest individual score to date when he won the individual competition in 2001. During that span he also co-authored *The Macmillan Baseball Quiz Book* and penned *The McFarland Baseball Quiz Book*. In addition, he has written numerous quizzes for independent publications.

In 1991, Scott received a call from Steve Nadel, the New York City SABR chapter chairman and host of that year's National convention in New York City, informing him that David Nemec was planning to attend a SABR convention for the first time. Scott immediately contacted me and we both became very excited because David is recognized to be the father of baseball trivia. He had written two books in the late 1970s, *The Absolutely Most Challenging Baseball Quiz Book, Ever* and *The Even More Challenging Baseball Quiz Book*, that are now regarded as the pioneering works in the field. Scott and I first met David in June of 1991 at the SABR New York City National convention for which Scott orchestrated the trivia competition. As a first-time player, David helped his team to narrowly defeat my team in the finals, and an instant bond developed between us.

In addition to *The Absolutely Most Challenging Baseball Quiz Book, Ever* and *The Even More Challenging Baseball Quiz Book*, David is the author of more than 25 baseball books including two quiz books in the 1990s, the indispensable *The Great Encyclopedia of Nineteenth Century Major League Baseball* and *The Beer and Whisky League*, which ranks as the seminal work on the American Association in the years that it was a major league. David is also the co-holder with me of a record seven SABR National Trivia Championships. He has won six team competitions as well as the first individual championship in 1995.

The matchless qualities in David Nemec's and Scott Flatow's new series of team quiz books are their wry wit, their amazing scope, and, above all, the fact that they not only test a reader's recall, they also force him or her to think out of the box and in so doing to expand his or her knowledge of our national game. You will never find such tired posers as "Who pitched the only perfect game in the World Series?" or "What year did the Dodgers move to Los Angeles?" Instead you will be constantly challenged to test the depth and breadth of your baseball knowledge from the first major league baseball game in 1871 to the present day. Furthermore, in this unique series of quiz books you are certain to learn a wealth of new information about players ranging from the well known like Babe Ruth and Hank Aaron to such inimitably ephemeral performers as Eddie Gaedel and Shooty Babbit.

In short, Nemec and Flatow inform as well as entertain. Most other quiz books are content to lob questions at you without helping to guide you toward the answer. You either know who hit such and such, or you don't. Your only recourse if you don't is to consult the answer section, shrug, and move on. Nemec and Flatow take a very different approach. First they toss a tantalizing and oftentimes completely original teaser to set your synapses firing. Then they crank your brain up to full boil with descriptive clues that are deftly designed to steer the savvy mind toward the answer. And fair warning: the answer is all too often a name that will make you whack your forehead and go, "Wow, how did I ever miss that?" Have fun with these books. I never had so much fun in all my long years as a trivia aficionado.

Alan Blumkin is the only man to win two consecutive individual SABR National trivia championships. In addition, he has made numerous historical presentations at both local and National SABR conventions. He lives in Brooklyn, New York, and is currently resting on his laurels while serving as the chief administrator and question contributor for the annual SABR National championships.

INTRODUCTION

How dare we call this the ultimate Boston Red Sox baseball challenge?

First and foremost, it's been designed to give you, our dear reader, the four things you most want in a baseball quiz book: (1) pleasure; (2) a worthy challenge; (3) an opportunity to learn something new about the game you love and the team that, chances are, many of you find at once endearing and eternally frustrating; (4) the assurance that you're in the company of quiz masters who know their stuff. In short, you not only want to match wits, you also like to come away from a book like this with the feeling that you've been enlightened in the bargain. You will be, you have our guarantee, by the time you finish here.

What we've assembled is a seven-game World Series of entertainment, innings one through nine, starting off with rookies and ending with famous Fall Classic events and heroes. There's a logic to our structure, of course, as there is to all the categories we've chosen. In fact, we'll alert you right off the bat, as it were, that to score well against our curves, drops, and heat you need to be moderately savvy in every on-the-field phase of the BoSox' rich history: from the early years of the franchise, when the team was known more commonly as the Americans, to the final pitch delivered last season.

That isn't to say, though, that you've got to have a raft of stats and a host of obscure players at your fingertips. Actually, top marks are there for the taking by anyone who has a reasonable amount of knowledge of the game in general coupled with a good eye for using our clues to zero in on the right answer to even our seemingly all but impossible questions. And speaking of stats, our authority for those we use is the current edition of *The*

ESPN Baseball Encyclopedia except in the very rare instances where that reference work conflicts with the authors' own research findings. Similarly, our authorities for issues like what constitutes rookie status, batting title eligibility, and other such matters are the current major league rules except in cases where we've alerted you that a different criterion is being used.

Before ushering you behind the curtain and showing you how our minds work, first let us show you an example of the type of question we abhor: What Kansas City Royals batter hit into the first triple play in Seattle Mariners history and what Mariner recorded the last out in the play? Unless you happened to see that particular play (which is highly unlikely) or else have a PhD in triple plays (also unlikely), all you can do is throw up your hands and take a couple of wild guesses as to who the two players are. And where's the fun in that? However, if the question had also provided the clues that the Royals batter now resides in the Hall of Fame and the Mariner who recorded the last out in the triple play spent most of his career as a backup catcher in the mid-1970s with the Astros, then all the burners would be fired and the question would be a fair one to ask, albeit still not one to our taste.

In short, that's our approach. A good question doesn't just toss up a mildly interesting but essentially arcane feat. It gives you a reasonable opportunity to nail the player or players who were involved in it by providing enough information about them to allow you to make at least an educated guess. Hall of Famer? Could be Harmon Killebrew who finished his career in KC. But wait! Was Killebrew still around when the Mariners came into existence? No. Then who was? We won't spoil the fun by giving away the answer any more than we'll spill on the 'stros backup catcher, but now you get the idea how we work.

Here we are cobbling away in our workshop on three different levels of questions that are more to our taste:

SIMPLE: Who is the only Red Sox bat titlist to log a 400+ batting average? Single.

INTERMEDIATE: It'll pester you all night if you don't know the only Red Sox swinger to date who collected 200 or more hits in each of his first three seasons with the club, especially after we add that he achieved this super feat in his first three seasons in the majors. Double.

EXPERT: In 1950 the Red Sox were blessed with four batting-title qualifiers who hit .322 or better. For one base, name the one that led the club that year in runs. Collect a second base if you know which one of the four had the most RBI. Yet a third base is yours for knowing the member of the quartet who won the AL batting title that year. Score a fourth base, plus two RBI if you know the only member of the quartet who had previously qualified for a ML bat title with a .322+ BA.

Question 1 is so easy that it merits no clues and rates only a single.

In question 2 you're given fair warning that the wording itself contains clues when the question is read carefully. Good for you if you've already spotted that our clues sometimes come in the form of wordplay or puns.

The reward in question 3 is among the highest offered in our book—the equivalent of a three-run homer. In addition, you get a sampling of the standard abbreviations we use. Here they're ML, short for major league, AL, short for American League, and BA, short for batting average. Elsewhere you'll encounter other standard abbreviations such as NL for National League, PCL for Pacific Coast League, AB for at bats, OBP for on base percentage, SA for slugging average, ERA for earned run average, OPS for on base percentage plus slugging average, and PA for plate appearances.

We won't spoil your fun by giving away the answers to our sample questions. Consider them a bonus. And, incidentally, there are a number of other bonuses in our book, not the least of which is our invitation to compile your own BA, SA, and RBI total as you go along. There are roughly 900 plate appearances in *The*

Ultimate Boston Red Sox Baseball Challenge. Don't expect to hit above .300, though, unless you really know your Crimson Hose. But by the same token, you have our assurance that not even die-hard Hub fans are likely to outhit readers who have a firm knowledge of all of major league history. This, after all, is the ultimate Red Sox test for the ultimate well-rounded fan.

Now enjoy.

GAME 1

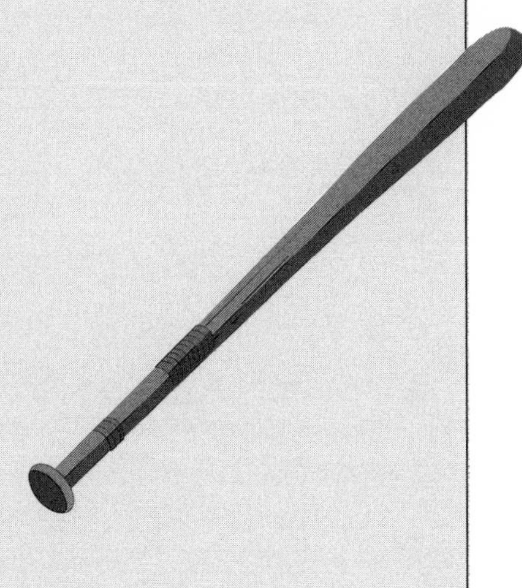

INNING 1
RED-HOT ROOKIES

1 We're wheeling out the charity wagon by asking you for the Crimson Hose hurler who led AL freshmen in wins, winning percentage, starts, innings, complete games, strikeouts, and ERA in 1915. A blindfolded single.

2 He tagged 34 taters as a BoSox rookie but only 152 total in a career that lasted some 13 seasons. He also collected more than a fifth of his career RBI total of 704 as a yearling. Who is he for a RBI single?

3 You deserve a pat on the back for naming the BoSox rookie record holder for highest BA (minimum 400 at bats). In 1902 this outfielder placed among the league BA leaders at .342 and also topped AL rooks in hits, runs, walks, steals, SA, and OBP. Dealt to the New York Highlanders during the 1904 campaign, he became the first performer to play regularly for both Boston and New York in the junior loop. Two-run triple.

4 Baseball's men in charge ruled that he wasn't a rookie in 1957. Though he violently disagreed, he lost the top AL frosh honor that year to Tony Kubek, who had a markedly less auspicious season. Who was this bereaved BoSoxer who would have been a rookie by today's rules? Two bases.

5 Born in Brockton, Mass., and exiting in the Hub, he first appeared in Sox garb on September 9, 1911, and proceeded to win five games before the season was out, combined with a microscopic 0.38 ERA. The following year, in his first full season, he won 20 games for the 1912 champs. Sadly, he won only four more before departing. Who was this frosh flash for a triple?

6 The Sox had a second yearling hurler who bagged 20 wins in 1912. After two so-so years in 1913 and 1914, he jumped to the

Federal League and led the rebel loop in saves with 10. The winner of 59 games in his brief four-year stint in the show, he rates a RBI triple.

7 In a lean year for rookie moundsmen, a certain bespectacled 6'4" Boston righty led ML yearlings with just nine wins as a starter-reliever in 1956. Two years later this son of a Hall of Famer yielded 22 homers in only 149⅓ innings before moving elsewhere during the following campaign. RBI double.

8 In 1956 the Sox sported a newbie infielder who topped AL freshmen in doubles and walks. Twice he led the junior loop in errors at his position, and by the winter of 1961 the BoSox had shipped him to the Colt .45s for his replacement, Eddie Bressoud. Two-run triple.

9 After a brief trial the year before in the NL, this lefty stick was still officially a rook when he pounded 21 seat-reachers with 73 RBI for the BoSox despite missing over 50 games. Though he was primarily seen at first base, Sox fans also saw him DH and roam the pasture. Single, plus a RBI for the year.

10 He had 46 wins after his first two seasons in the bigs, the fastest start ever by a Sox hurler. Yet he won his 65th and last ML game when he was just 26. Don't let us scare you—this isn't some obscure Deadballer. Two-bagger.

11 Called up in late September after batting .334 at Pawtucket, he set an all-time rookie mark by collecting hits in his first six trips to the plate in BoSox garb and stroked a wicked .362 in 58 at bats. Named MVP of the International League that year, he never again played with Boston and did little else during his five-year big league journey. Single, plus a RBI for his flashy debut year.

12 In 1930 a rookie center fielder led the BoSox in games, at bats, hits, and runs and rapped a solid .293 while fanning only 25 times. Okay, it was seemingly solid. To this day, his .293 BA is the highest ever by a Sox gardener who compiled a sub-.700 OPS (minimum 500 PA). In 1933 he wrapped up his four-year career, all in Boston garb, with a .277 career BA but just a .656 OPS.

The clue that our rook holds the post-1900 record for the most career at bats (1,931) without ever hitting a home run shakes this down to a RBI double.

13 The youngest Sox pitcher since expansion to log a double-figure-win season turned 21 less than three weeks before earning his 10th and final victory of his freshman campaign. Although he started over 90 games by age 23, he closed with just 134 career starts and only 177 total hill appearances. Double, plus a RBI for his frosh year.

14 Prior to expansion, Sox rookie first-base stars traditionally flopped in their second seasons. Who broke the mold in 1952–1953 when he hit 19 home runs as a rookie and followed by tagging 21 as a soph? RBI double.

15 His 2.18 ERA in 1909, his official rookie season, proved to be the worst he ever posted in a campaign in which he pitched enough to qualify for an ERA crown by today's rules. Who is this Sox hill great for a RBI double?

AB: 15
Hits: 15
Total Bases: 30
RBI: 13

INNING 2
WHAT WAS THEIR REAL HANDLE?

Ted Williams's real first name was Theodore and Yaz's was Carl, but the mothers of the Soxers in this category never intended for their sons to be called the names by which they became known to baseball fans everywhere.

1 Roger Clemens. RBI single.

2 Ike Delock. Triple.

3 Moose Grimshaw. Two-run homer.

4 Moose Solters. Two-run triple.

5 Rico Petrocelli. Single.

6 Milt Gaston. Three-run homer.

7 Bobo Newsom. RBI double.

8 Butch Hobson. Double.

9 Buck Freeman. Two-run double.

10 Pete Runnels. Double.

11 Buddy Myer. Two-bagger.

12 Jake Jones. Home run.

13 Mickey McDermott. RBI double.

14 Pumpsie Green. Two-run double.

15 Coco Crisp. RBI single.

AB: 15
Hits: 15
Total Bases: 35
RBI: 16

INNING 3
MASTER MOUNDSMEN

1 Who posted the highest season strikeout to walk ratio (8.88) in Red Sox history among hurlers who logged at least one inning per team game played? Single, plus a RBI for the year.

2 The antithesis of the previous hurler, in his 10-year career, all of it spent with the Sox, he walked 758 batters while fanning just 732. Yet, despite this seemingly horrible ratio, he finished with a .621 career winning percentage. Deadball guy? Think again. RBI double.

3 Cy Young won over 25 games in Boston livery for the fourth straight time in 1904. Who would be the next Sox hurler to bag a 25+ win season? RBI double.

4 Who was the most recent twirler to log a 25-win season for the BoSox? Single for him, RBI for his big year when he topped the AL in victories.

5 Who was the only pitcher since Cy Young in 1902 to win as many as 25 games for a BoSox club that was not still in the pennant race on the last day of the season? Two-run double, plus an extra RBI for his big year when he paced the AL in wins.

6 The first Soxer to win over 15 games for three straight seasons since the days of Mel Parnell might come as a surprise, so we're awarding a triple off the Green Monster for this practitioner of the palm ball.

7 The only BoSoxer since World War II to pitch at least one inning per team game played and post an ERA below 3.00 while suffering a sub-.500 record did it with a Crimson Hose flag winner. He quietly led all qualifiers on that club with a 2.77 ERA as a starter and spot reliever, yet logged only an 8–10 slate. Easy to get stung here, so we'll go for a bases clearing double.

8 Five southpaws have bagged 20-win seasons in Sox garb. Name this quintet for a solo homer. Single if you know just four.

9 He won AL Comeback Player of the Year honors and became the first Sox starter ever to notch as many as 15 victories in a season in which he failed to complete a single game. A shadow of his former self when he hit Boston, this former ace's potential Hall of Fame career was destroyed by injuries. Single, plus a RBI for his super comeback year.

10 Who logged the most career games to date by a southpaw in Sox garb? Many forget this lefty worked primarily from the pen during his first four Fenway campaigns before becoming a starter. RBI single.

11 What six-time 20-game winner went 13–11 for the 1906 Sox cellar club that was 36–94 on days when he didn't take the hill? Clues are right for a two-run triple.

12 Which one of these mound performers never led a Red Sox club in victories? Hideo Nomo, Eddie Cicotte, Earl Wilson, Bob Kline, Willard Nixon. RBI single.

13 A certain Sox lefty held the AL season record for 54 years for holding opposing batters to the lowest BA until another chucker, who later starred for the BoSox, broke the ML mark with a rival AL outfit. Not to be outdone, a third hurler narrowly bested this all-time standard while sporting Fenway flannels. Sort out the clues here, put the correct name to each hurler we've depicted, and grab a homer for all three, double for two, naught for anything less.

14 This one will cause brainlock in many of our readers, guaranteed. Who is the only hurler prior to AL expansion in 1961 to appear in as many as 250 games for the BoSox and pitch fewer than 1,000 innings? RBI double.

AB: 14
Hits: 14
Total Bases: 29
RBI: 18

INNING 4
GOLD GLOVE GOLIATHS

1 What newbie regular was the sole Red Sox Gold Glove recipient in 1957, the year the award was first given? Single for him, gift RBI for his position.

2 This Sox star copped four Gold Gloves by age 28 but never won another thereafter. Single, plus a RBI for the year he snagged his first fielding award.

3 Some Sox fans might pause before naming the club's sole second sacker to earn a Gold Glove. Dogged by injuries including back spasms, broken hands, and a beaning, he never played enough to qualify for the bat crown after earning top fielding honors at age 25. Double, plus a RBI for his award-winning year.

4 At age 23 he became the youngest Sox glove man to date to earn fielding ingot honors and also topped the majors in putouts at his position that season. Although he played for years in both leagues and appeared in seven All-Star contests, he never won another Gold Glove. Single, plus a RBI for the year.

5 Identify the oldest Soxer to win a Gold Glove and earn yourself a bloop single. Take an extra base for the year he won his last fielding bullion, plus a RBI for knowing his age by season's end.

6 This shortstop won eight straight AL fielding average crowns—six of them with Boston—and is credited by *The ESPN Baseball Encyclopedia* with over 100 fielding runs. He broke in with the Sox the same year the Babe made his debut with them and finished with Cincinnati in 1926. Two bases.

7 He won two AL Gold Gloves as a center fielder—one with Boston—but his best leather year may have been 1956, the year before the Gold Glove originated, when he led all junior-loop gardeners in putouts and FA. RBI single.

8 The whopping increase in strikeouts since expansion has resulted in mushrooming putout totals by catchers. Name the only backstopper in the top 25 on the Sox list for the most receivers' putouts in a season that achieved his total prior to expansion. Moreover, he appears on the list twice for back-to-back seasons in which the Sox finished fourth. RBI double.

9 What BoSox freshman won a Gold Glove but never earned another thereafter? We're not talking about some flash in the pan here. Believe it or not, he played more seasons in the majors than Carl Yastrzemski! Single, plus a RBI for the year he bagged his lone bullion.

10 What receiver has held the Sox season record for the most assists by a catcher since Day One of the club's existence? Double. For two RBI, name the year he set the current season standard of 156.

11 Not only does this hurler hold the Sox record for the most assists in a season by a moundsman, but he's also the lone Crimson Hoser to log 100 or more assists in three straight seasons. He won 20 in both leagues and pitched on flag winners in two different AL cities, his first such experience coming with Boston. RBI single.

12 A year after earning his leather bullion, this BoSoxer participated in 147 double plays, a record for his position. Never a big run producer, he did rap over .290 in consecutive seasons in Crimson Hose. Double.

13 Ted Williams places seventh on the Sox list for most career outfield assists. Who ranks first with 260? True team historians will bank an easy single.

14 The lone shortstop in Sox history to help turn over 100 double plays in three consecutive seasons did it in the only three seasons with the club in which he played 100 or more games in the field. Two bases for him, plus a RBI for his three-year span.

AB: 14
Hits: 14
Total Bases: 21
RBI: 12

INNING 5
RBI RULERS

1 Buck Freeman topped the Sox in RBI in each of their first four years of existence. What former NL star broke his stranglehold on the team leadership with a lowly 65 RBI in 1905 when the club fell from first to fourth place? Two-bagger.

2 After driving in 108 Astros, this hot-tempered hitter matched that total the next season and led the Sox to become the first ambidextrous swinger in ML history to reach the ribby century mark in *consecutive* years while playing in two different leagues. Swapped for Darren Oliver the following campaign, he's good for a single, plus a RBI for the season he chased home over 100 Sox mates.

3 What Sox slugger holds the ML season record for the most RBI by a player with a sub-.300 BA? Sounds like a post-expansion swinger, but telling you he isn't should help direct you to a double. Take a RBI for the year, plus an extra base for knowing his lofty ribby total.

4 Shoot a single through the middle by naming the first Soxer since Teddy Ballgame to collect 100+ RBI while hitting .350 or better. Snag a ribby of your own for pegging the year.

5 Who was the Sox career RBI leader with 629 prior to the arrival of Jimmie Foxx? Double.

6 Buck Freeman was the first Red Sox rapper to achieve a 100 RBI season. After a long dearth, who became the second in 1912? Two-bagger.

7 Buck Freeman was also the first Soxer to top the AL in RBI. Who was the club's next loop RBI leader and what year did he do it? You need both the man and the year for a RBI double.

8 Among players with at least 500 PA in a season, he had the lowest RBI total of any Soxer when he brought home just 24 mates in 504 trips to the plate. Remarkably he was not a Deadballer or a middle infielder. What's more, after this disastrous showing the Sox dumped him during the offseason and celebrated by winning the pennant the following year. Double.

9 Ted Williams was the first BoSox bammer to pace the AL in RBI three times. Who later tied his club mark with three AL RBI titles? RBI single.

10 The first BoSox middle infielder to notch 100 RBI did it in a season in which he tagged only five home runs. Triple for him, plus a RBI for his breakthrough season.

11 In 1930 the Red Sox finished last and scored just 612 runs while the rest of the AL averaged 865. Who led the 1930 club with a mere 66 RBI and also topped them in homers with 16? Triple.

12 The first BoSox club with more than one 100-RBI man had no fewer than three. Name the club for a double, plus two RBI if you know all three 100-RBI men.

13 Who broke the Sox career mark for RBI by a switch-hitter when he drove in his 537th run? Just a single.

14 Awarded AL Comeback Player of the Year, he responded the following campaign with a team-leading 116 RBI. The Sox rewarded his achievements by dealing him away, but sadly he proved them right by totaling just 15 ribbies that season before retiring. Returning four years later on a Sox flag winner, he had his ill-advised comeback attempt end after just 27 games. Single.

AB: 14
Hits: 14
Total Bases: 26
RBI: 8

INNING 6
TEAM TEASERS

1 What was the first major league park to be used for home games by the Red Sox franchise in more than one World Series? No trickery here—it's a fact and you're up for a double.

2 The first BoSox outfit that featured three players who clubbed at least 30 jacks apiece won 97 games but still placed second in the AL East. Score a double for the year and a RBI for each of the sluggers.

3 From April 1929 until May 1932 the Sox played all their Sunday home games in Braves Field. Tell us why and win a solo shot over the Green Monster.

4 What Sox club had among its nine position players in 100 or more games the following names? Charlie Berry, Urbane Pickering, Al Van Camp, Otto Miller, and Bill Sweeney.

5 Discounting strike years, the club that holds the post-expansion record for fewest steals in a season is the habitually lumbering BoSox. Single for the year.

6 What was the first BoSox club to hit 100 or more dingers in a season? Sounds hard, but a bit of sly thinking will put you in the right era. RBI triple.

7 This Sox squad was 6½ games out of first by the end of June but climbed into the top spot by late July, closing with a club-record 25 wins that month. Regrettably, they fell short of the flag despite winning 39 of their last 60. Double for this dogged crew.

8 What was the first Sox squad to draw 2 million fans at home during a season in which they finished with a sub-.500 record? Knowing a bit about what historically spikes team attendance from the previous year should help guide you to a single.

9 The Sox set a ML record in 1949 that was entirely in keeping with what was going on in the AL that year. What was that record? Triple.

10 What was the only BoSox club to tally as many as 200 steals in a season? The arrival of a speedster from Texas had much to do with the club's swiping 215 sacks. Two-run triple.

11 What was the first Red Sox club to post a 5.00+ ERA while logging a winning record? They won 85 games, finishing just seven games off the pace while scoring 928 runs and allowing just seven fewer markers to cross the plate. RBI single.

12 The last Red Sox pitching core to notch as many as 100 complete games achieved it in a season when the staff as a whole made only 126 starts! That clue alone should steer you to a double.

13 What Sox team was led in hits, runs, home runs, total bases, RBI, batting average, slugging average, and on base percentage by a forgotten figure in Boston who had his best year since his 1929 frosh campaign with Detroit? Triple for the team; two-run homer if you also know the player.

14 In what year did the BoSox set the team season record for victories? Despite winning over 90 games, the second-place Senators finished 14 games behind the Crimson Hose that season. RBI single.

AB: 14
Hits: 14
Total Bases: 33
RBI: 13

INNING 7
HOME RUN KINGS

1 The first bammer to lead the AL in homers played for the initial Boston team to take the field as a member of the junior circuit. Two bases for the 1901 AL home run king.

2 In his lone season with the Sox, this first sacker led them with 30 homers and 108 RBI but never again hit another tater or drove in a single run. After he signed a fat free-agent deal with Ted Turner's Braves, an inner-ear infection caused vertigo, ending his career at age 30. Double, plus a RBI for his big season.

3 Between Babe Ruth's ill-fated swap to the Yankees and the arrival of Jimmie Foxx, who was the only BoSox swatter to finish among the top five in the AL in homers? Triple, plus two RBI for the year he finished fifth with 13 taters.

4 What Sox gardener compiled the fewest homers in a season by a club leader since World War II? Decimated by injuries, the entire team managed just 84 dingers, with this Covina, Calif., clubber leading the way with a paltry 15 in 458 at bats. After exiting as a free agent, he returned to Boston in a straight-up swap with the Brewers for catcher Dave Valle. Double.

5 In the decade of the 1950s (1951–1960) the Sox had no AL home run champs and only three top-five finishers. One was Walt Dropo, but the other two finished among the top five more than once, and you need both for a two-bagger.

6 Who was the first BoSox receiver to lead the club in homers? Poke this meatball through our wickets for a single, plus a RBI for the year.

7 Who held the Sox pre-expansion mark for the most career home runs by a switch-hitter with a mere 14? He patrolled the outfield in Fenway from 1925 until early in the 1932 season and rates a home run.

8 Which of these men never led a BoSox team in homers? Nomar Garciaparra, Mike Greenwell, Bobby Doerr, Vern Stephens, Del Pratt, Harry Hooper. Single.

9 Who broke Babe Ruth's Red Sox club record for most career home runs when he hit his 50th career tater in his last year in Sox raiment? RBI triple.

10 Among players with at least 500 plate appearances, who holds the Sox season mark for highest BA while hitting fewer than 10 homers? He copped the bat title that campaign by 33 points, so we can't in good conscience offer more than a single, plus a RBI for the year.

11 Who was the only BoSoxer prior to AL expansion in 1961 to smack over 10 homers two years in a row while hitting under .250 in both seasons? Triple.

12 It might surprise you to learn the name of the outfielder that poled the most homers in a season for the Sox from 1990 through 1999. In his big year he led the club with 28 seat-reachers, the most by a BoSox pasture patroller since Dwight Evans in 1985. Initially a steal for Boston after being claimed on waivers from Milwaukee, he sank fast when the club squandered over $8 million on his services. RBI single.

13 The AL record for the most at bats in a season without snaring at least one home run is 658. What BoSox gardener holds it? Even experts are liable to spout the name of the wrong Sox flychaser here. RBI triple.

14 Who was the first Sox middle infielder to hit 20 homers and steal 20 bases in a season? In parts of 10 Beantown seasons he pounded over 100 round-trippers, but by his early thirties his numbers plummeted, and after a few injury-plagued seasons he never recovered enough to play regularly again. RBI single, plus an extra base for his standout season.

AB: 14
Hits: 14
Total Bases: 30
RBI: 10

INNING 8
STELLAR STICKWIELDERS

1 Who was the Red Sox first AL bat champ? Double for him, plus a ribby for his triumphant year.

2 In stroking .326, this infielder not only posted the highest season BA in Sox history by a switch-hitting batting-title qualifier, but he also copped the AL hitting crown. Single, plus a RBI for the year.

3 How many times combined did Ted Williams and Wade Boggs lead the AL in hits? RBI single.

4 Name the first Boston AL bammer to pace the junior loop in total bases. RBI double.

5 What Soxer is the only ALer to lead in doubles twice without ever hitting 40 two-baggers in a season? Across seven seasons as a regular, this pastureman drilled over 200 doubles in crimson garb before moving to the NL. Net two of your own for this Louisiana lasher.

6 Who was the first stickwielder to win two bat crowns in Sox clothes? Single for him, plus a RBI for his first two victory seasons.

7 In 1983 he set the Sox season record for highest BA by a pinch stick (minimum 30 at bats), skewering opposing pitchers at a .457 clip. Quietly he hung around the big league scene for 15 years, with 12 of them coming in Boston. Double.

8 Who is the only Sox catcher besides Carlton Fisk to slug .500+ in a season? That year this backstop poked 25 homers, plus 31 doubles and 85 RBI in 142 games. Single, plus a RBI for the year.

9 What Sox bammer set a club record in 1953 for the lowest season slugging average by a performer with at least 20 home runs? RBI double.

10 In 1954 Bobby Avila of Cleveland won the AL bat crown. What Sox stickman would have won it according to current eligibility rules? Single.

11 When Yaz won the 1968 AL bat title, whose club record did he break for the lowest BA to win the crown? RBI single, plus an extra base for the year our man won with a .320 mark.

12 Who was the first Crimson Hose swinger to slash 200 hits for three straight seasons? Set your sights on this slugger who totaled a league-leading 213, sandwiched between seasons of 206 and 201. Single, plus a RBI for his three-year run.

13 When Ted Williams led the AL for the first time in total bases, what was unique about his victory? RBI double.

14 The second youngest player in AL history to garner 2,000 hits did it in Red Sox garb. Who is he for a deuce? Take a RBI for the year he did it.

15 The first Red Sox performer to top the AL in slugging average was a lefty hitter who now resides in Cooperstown. RBI single, plus an extra base for the year he did it.

AB: 15
Hits: 15
Total Bases: 22
RBI: 12

INNING 9
FALL CLASSICS

1 Wouldn't you know it, but the most recent lefty to beat the BoSox at Fenway in World Series play began his career in Red Sox flannels. Double for this turncoat.

2 The first AL hitter to step to the plate in a so-called "modern" World Series game wore a Boston uniform, as we all should know. Name him for a two-bagger.

3 In 17 big league seasons, primarily in the pasture, he played for eight AL clubs but saw Series action in just one of those campaigns. However, skipper Darrell Johnson penciled him into the leadoff spot in the starting lineup for Game 5 in 1975. A native of Puerto Rico, he's solid for two.

4 What gardener led Boston in hits and BA in the 1903 Series? He occupied center field and batted in the third spot in the order. Single.

5 Cy Young and Bill Dinneen hurled 69 of the 71 innings that were played in the 1903 Series. The other two frames came from what righty who started Game 3 and was removed after the second inning trailing 3–0? Three-run three-bagger.

6 In Game 6 of the 1967 Series, Boston became the first club to launch three homers in one inning. Take a triple for naming their seat-reaching trio, but a single for knowing only two.

7 The Red Sox belted four home runs in the 1946 World Series. The only team member to hit two also led the club in runs with six and RBI with five despite hitting just .261. RBI double.

8 Boston's only two home runs in its first World Series appearance in 1903 came off the bat of the same player—and in the same game no less! RBI single.

9 You'll get burned for forgetting the name of the BoSox swinger who tied the current Series mark with two pinch-hit homers. Single.

10 What BoSoxer once slapped a Series record-tying 13 hits en route to a .433 BA and would almost certainly have been named the classic's MVP had Boston emerged victorious? RBI single.

11 The BoSox got two complete-game wins in the 1946 World Series. One came from the club's Series leader in strikeouts with 10 and also in ERA with a perfect 0.00 in 12⅔ innings. A long-time Sox mound stalwart, he's seldom mentioned today. Three bases.

12 Hold your nose, Sox fans, and cough up the name of the former Met who infamously lost Game 6 for Boston in the 1986 Series. Single.

13 The demoralized losing pitcher in Game 7 of the 1946 World Series was making his lone career fall appearance that afternoon. Fasten on to the clue that he was a reliever with the 1946 club after a long NL career as a starter and score a RBI triple.

14 Who played in all four Series games for the triumphant BoSox in 2004 but never again appeared in a big league game? Poke this one up the middle for a single.

AB: 14
Hits: 14
Total Bases: 26
RBI: 7

GAME 2

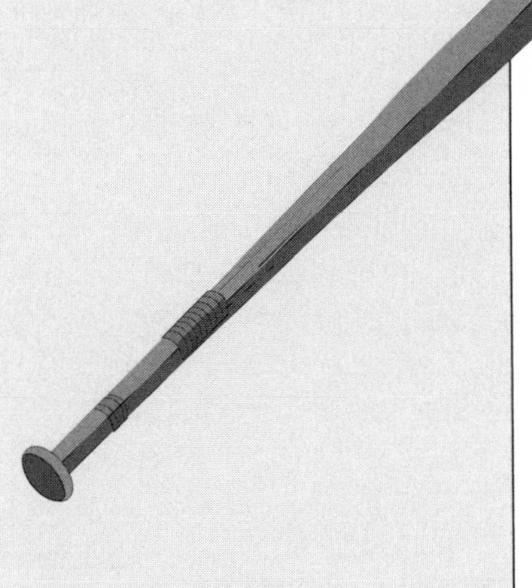

INNING 1
STELLAR STICKWIELDERS

1 Among Sox stickmen who were at least 40 years old, which one posted the highest season SA with a minimum of 400 plate appearances? Single, plus a RBI for this golden oldie's silver year.

2 Who was the first Boston AL performer to garner as many as 300 total bases in a season? One base for him, an extra sack for the year he did it.

3 What Boston-born middle infielder recently set the ML season mark for strikeouts by a switch-hitter but nonetheless compiled a fine .817 OPS and tallied 93 runs? Single, plus a RBI for the year he sawed the air in record fashion.

4 Who was the first Red Sox regular to post a .700+ season slugging average? One sack for him and a RBI for the year he did it.

5 Just one Sox clubber has pounded at least 40 homers in a season without driving in 100 runs. However, the following year this performer whacked just 29 taters and sent home 103 mates, the only time he reached the century mark during his 13-year big league ride. Double, plus a RBI for the year he failed to drive in 100 despite all those bombs.

6 The first middle infielder to pace the AL in slugging average since the Deadball Era made Fenway his home park. Double for him, plus a RBI for the year he led.

7 Who was the first Red Sox regular to post a season OPS of 1.000 or better? One for him, plus a RBI for the year.

8 Among Soxers with 2,000+ PA, who posted the highest career OPS (.723) while hitting less than .250? He spent five seasons in the BoSox infield, playing at least 114 games each year, but lasted just one more campaign thereafter as a Tigers and Astros sub. RBI double.

9 Who was the only Sox swinger to hit below .300 in a season despite slapping over 200 hits? Never one to coax walks throughout his 22 seasons up top, he drew just 30 free passes that year, setting the club record for lowest season OBP (.325) by a 200-hit man. Double, plus a RBI for the year.

10 Ted Williams was the first Red Sox stickman to pace the AL in walks outright. What Soxer had previously tied for the AL lead one year in free passes? Double for him, plus a RBI for the year he shared the lead with that season's ML home run king.

11 When this smooth lefty swinger hit Fenway, he had already copped an AL bat crown, stroked over 2,000 hits, and sported two World Series championship rings. More interestingly, he had never played in the minors until a brief stint in Pawtucket preceded his BoSox debut. Single, plus a RBI for what proved to be his coda campaign.

12 Three Soxers slugged .600+ in a season despite drilling fewer than 30 homers. The Babe was the first, and Teddy Ballgame—the second—did it five times. Who was the third man to do it? Grab a single, plus a RBI for the year.

13 The player who holds the documented Sox season mark for the fewest strikeouts (22) combined with a 200-hit campaign is the only BoSox performer to date to fan fewer than 30 times, twice while rapping 200 hits. Double, plus a RBI for his record-setting year.

14 When Tris Speaker became the first Red Sox hitter to lead the AL in doubles in 1912, what was significant about his total? Two-bagger.

AB: 14
Hits: 14
Total Bases: 22
RBI: 12

INNING 2
MASTER MOUNDSMEN

1 The Sox record holder for the most wins in a season with 34 also set a new all-time record that year that lasted until 1931. He's just a single, but the all-time record he once held rates three RBI. P.S.: Prior to our Sox ace, the record had belonged to Baltimore's Bill Hoffer, who set it in 1895.

2 Prior to Pedro Martinez's arrival, who held the Red Sox club mark for highest career winning percentage (minimum 50 decisions)? A starter-reliever, this side-arming southpaw once reeled off 11 straight victories, and if you add his two best Sox seasons together, you get a phenomenal 27–5 slate. Double.

3 Among southpaws who worked a minimum of 1,000 innings with the Sox and notched more than 50 decisions, who has the highest career winning percentage? RBI double.

4 What Hall of Famer won in double figures in each of his only two seasons in Fenway? Though he's seldom associated with the Sox, he led the club with 11 complete games in the latter campaign despite logging only 10 wins. Our sharing that this well-traveled righty was born north of the U.S. border and led both the NL and AL in wins at one time or another should help you to a single.

5 Including all hurlers who pitched one inning per team game played, the Sox season record for the best ERA by a qualifier belongs to a certain southpaw. Name him for a single, plus a RBI for his super season.

6 Since the end of the Deadball Era in 1919, the Sox have had only one lefty slab man bag an AL ERA crown. Well, more than one crown actually. His 2.54 ERA in one of his winning seasons also stands as the Sox post-Deadball southpaw mark. He's a single, but knowing how many ERA titles he took while with Boston will bring two extra bases.

7 Among hurlers who averaged at least one inning per team game, which one registered the first, second, and fourth best seasons in terms of fewest hits allowed per nine innings by a Red Sox lefty since the end of the Deadball Era in 1919? The answer here will surprise many but not batters who faced him. Two-run double.

8 The first Sox lefty since the close of the Deadball Era to allow fewer than eight hits per nine innings was an AL All-Star selection in 1943, the year he was touched for just 7.59 hits per every nine frames. He won only one more game for the Sox after that season but did some good work with the Phils after World War II. Score a two-run four-bagger if you know this southpaw who did not win his first ML game until he was 34.

9 Among Sox pitchers who logged one inning per team game played, Cy Young has a death grip on the top five seasons for fewest walks allowed per nine innings. Who occupies the sixth slot as a result of allowing just 1.03 walks per nine frames the year after the Sox won it all? We'll add that he is a lefty and award you a single, plus a RBI for the year.

10 Who issued the fewest walks in a season by a Sox 20-game winner since the close of the Deadball Era? He topped the AL in victories with 21 that campaign and issued just 35 free passes. Single, plus a RBI for the year.

11 Who are the only two hurlers that can claim credit for performing all three of these feats while members of the Red Sox? A .600+ Sox career winning percentage, at least 100 Hub wins, never on a Sox flag winner. You need both to score a RBI triple.

12 Whose 19 wins led the only Sox World Series–bound club to date that did not feature at least one 20-game winner? Double.

13 The last hurler in Red Sox history to log as many as 300 innings in a 154-game season did it in back-to-back years. He's a deuce, and his two seasons rate another base.

AB: 13
Hits: 13
Total Bases: 26
RBI: 12

INNING 3
CY YOUNG SIZZLERS

1 None other than Cy himself would have won the award named for him had it existed in the AL's inaugural season, as he posted 33 of Boston's 79 victories and led the junior loop in wins. What Hub slabster almost certainly would have copped the award in the AL the following year, when Boston slipped to just 77 wins? Two-bagger.

2 Don't expect more than a single for naming the first Red Sox Cy Young recipient. Interestingly, he never earned a single vote in any of his 14 other seasons up top.

3 What southpaw broke Cy Young's four-year stranglehold on the Sox club lead in wins in 1905 and might well have bagged that season's top AL pitching honor with his glittering 22–9 mark were it not for another lefty named Rube Waddell? Triple.

4 On a Sox club that won 93 games, he finished second in the AL in wins, ERA, and lowest opponents OBP but placed a distant third in the AL Cy Young race, failing to notch a single first-place vote. RBI single, plus an extra base for the year.

5 Bob Feller paced the AL in wins and Ks in 1946 but might well have lost the Cy Young honor to what BoSoxer whose 25–6 mark gave him a loop-leading .806 winning percentage? RBI single.

6 In the Cy Young Award's first five years of existence (1956–1960) no Boston hurler earned so much as a single vote for the honor. There was good reason for it—no Hub hillmen deserved a vote. Who was the only Sox twirler during that span to win as many as 15 games in a season? Two-run triple.

7 What BoSox chucker would have been the odds-on favorite had there been a Cy Young trophy in 1942 when he paced the AL with 22 wins and 281 innings? RBI double.

8 Wes Ferrell might have been a near unanimous Cy Young choice in 1935 when he topped the AL with 25 wins. What other Sox hurler would have garnered most of the votes that year that went elsewhere for his 20 wins and loop-leading 2.70 ERA? Two-run single.

9 Smokey Joe Wood topped the AL in 1912 with 34 wins and a .872 winning percentage. But Wood was by no means a lock to have won the loop's top pitching honor that year. Who would have given him stiff competition by dint of his 33 wins and AL-best 1.39 ERA? Single.

10 Who was the first Sox tosser to earn Cy Young votes in two different seasons? Actually, he stretched it to three such showings in five years and retired with 122 wins in Boston. RBI single.

11 The 1948 Red Sox lost the flag by only one game but lacked a 20-game winner or a viable Cy Young candidate. Whose 18–5 record and league-leading .783 winning percentage would have put him in the running were it not for his lackluster 4.35 ERA? Two-run triple.

12 With another ML outfit, he led the majors in relief wins with 10 six years before earning a Cy Young in Boston. Sharp single.

13 Following their 1946 flag win, in 1947 the Red Sox crashed when several of their top starters developed ailing arms. Who emerged as the club's go-to wing when he led the Sox in wins, ERA, and complete games? His 18–8 mark in 1947 would surely have garnered a fair amount of Cy Young support to boot. Three bases.

14 What Soxer finished third in the Cy Young balloting after spending the entire previous season in the minors? No rookie at the time, he was sent down by his former club to hone his control. Unfortunately, he collapsed in Triple A, leading the American Association in losses, walks, runs yielded, hits surrendered, homers allowed, and hit batsmen. Nevertheless, the Sox rescued him from the scrap heap and he rewarded them with a team-leading 16 wins, earning AL Comeback Player of the Year honors. Single for this true reclamation success story, plus a RBI for his triumphant return season.

AB: 14
Hits: 14
Total Bases: 25
RBI: 11

INNING 4
BULLPEN BLAZERS

1 Prior to AL expansion in 1961, the BoSox club record for the most career saves stood at 91. What hurler who once was a 20-game winner with the Sox held the mark? Two-bagger.

2 The last big league reliever to toss enough innings to qualify for the ERA title strictly for his pen work actually placed second in ERA to the Indians' Rick Sutcliffe. Single for this BoSox iron-man, plus a ribby for his super season.

3 Despite the heat displayed by today's power relievers, the way they are currently pampered makes it highly unlikely that anyone will eclipse this hulking Red Sox fireman's single-season relievers' strikeout record. Single for him, a RBI for the year, plus an extra base for knowing his whiff total within two.

4 Acquired from Philadelphia, he paced the Sox with 31 saves before wearing out his welcome by late July of the following season, when he was sent packing after notching 17 saves but coupled with a horrendous 5.79 ERA. Double for this uniquely named righty.

5 The Red Sox missed the boat on this future bullpen standout. From 1952 through 1955 they gave him a long look, mostly as a starter, before dispensing with his services and then watching him return to the majors three years later with the Cubs, strictly as a reliever. Death on left-handed bats, he remained one of the NL's dominant setup men and closers until he was past 40. RBI double for the lean lefty from Alice, Texas.

6 What former Pirates starter joined the Red Sox in 1946 and promptly led the AL in saves at age 38? He finished with the 1947 club, collecting a total of 14 saves in his 56 hill appearances with the Sox. RBI triple.

7 The first Boston AL hurler in history to record a save was also the team's biggest loser in its inaugural season. Plenty there to score a three-bagger.

8 The Sox have had five pitchers that both started and saved 10 games in the same season. Remarkably, four have done it since AL expansion. Name the lone hurler to perform this feat for the Sox prior to expansion and serve yourself a tasty two-run homer, plus an extra RBI for the year that he led not only the Sox but also the entire AL in saves.

9 A year after appearing in three World Series games against the Reds in 1975, he set the Sox single-season club mark with 12 relief losses but still managed to convert 10 of 13 save opportunities. Only the sheer force of will can earn you a RBI double here.

10 In 1939 the Sox finished second to perhaps the strongest New York Yankees club ever. What bullpen heaver posted a glittering 11–3 record and led the Sox in saves with seven? Two-run homer.

11 The initial BoSox pen man to post a 40-save season actually set the ML career record in that department in crimson threads, later broken. Oddly, in 2005 this former multimillionaire stopper who hailed from Dalton, Mass., was arrested for robbing a jewelry store with a gun. Single.

12 Not to be outdone by the above relief ace, this Sox closer, who also saved 40 one year, shifted from the bullpen to the holding pen after being sentenced to 14 years for attempted murder in his native Venezuela. A single for this Caracas kook.

13 Who was the most recent Sox reliever to lead the club in victories? Bagging 14 wins plus 14 saves, this righty would finish his five-year Boston sojourn without ever starting a game in 225 outings. Double, plus a RBI for his leadership year.

AB: 13
Hits: 13
Total Bases: 29
RBI: 11

INNING 5
WHO'D THEY COME UP WITH

Just about all of the Red Sox linchpins in this category cut their teeth with another major league team. Do you know the team whose threads they first wore? The initial year they appeared in the majors will earn two extra RBI.

1 Buck Freeman. Grand-slam homer.

2 Brian Daubach. RBI single.

3 Candy LaChance. Triple.

4 Gary Geiger. Double.

5 Joe Dobson. Two-run double.

6 Bill Dinneen. Triple.

7 Stan Spence. Double.

8 Hal Wagner. RBI triple.

9 Johnny Damon. Single.

10 Pete Runnels. RBI single.

11 Tony Armas. Tough triple.

12 Jake Jones. RBI triple.

13 Ellis Kinder. Two-run triple.

14 Pedro Martinez. Bad-hop single.

15 Dick Hoblitzel. RBI double.

AB: 15
Hits: 15
Total Bases: 34
RBI: 43

INNING 6
FAMOUS FEATS

1 What Soxer was the first switch-hitter in ML history to blast grand slams from both sides of the plate in the same game? Double.

2 Name the Crimson Hose tosser who holds the World Series record for fewest hits allowed in two consecutive complete games with a mere four. Our mouth-watering clue that three of those hits came in one start reduces this to a single.

3 The first Sox bammer to stroke three home runs in a contest did it in the second game of a July 4 doubleheader in his rookie season in the bigs. In the process, he also became the initial Soxer to knock two grand slams in the same game as well as the first to cream four homers in a doubleheader. He was nonetheless far from being the club's most vaunted rookie that season. Two-run homer if you name both him and the teammate who was the Hub's yearling standout. Zip for knowing only one of these frosh sensations.

4 What Sox Hall of Famer played for a different Crimson Hose skipper in each of his first three big league games? How is that possible? Here's how: In between his first two games, the initial skipper got canned, so in his second contest our performer played for an interim pilot. Then he waited two years for his next big league taste, and by that time another helmsman was holding the Sox reins. Take a double for nailing the Cooperstown inductee and a RBI for each of his first three skippers you can name.

5 The first member of the home team to crank three balls over Fenway barriers in the same game later had two other three-homer games, both coming on the road. His initial three-homer game came in the same year a Washington first sacker won the AL bat title. He's just a single, but the year is worth two RBI if you also know the Washington hitsmith who later served as the Sox regular gateway guardian.

6 Who was the youngest Red Sox pitcher to start on Opening Day? This lad won not only that game but also the next two Sox openers, only to never again take the hill for a season lid-lifter. Yet another arm burnout case? Nope. Piece the clues together for a RBI single, plus another ribby for the year of his initial Opening Day start.

7 What Soxer was the first DH to slap four doubles in one game? Although he played over 1,600 games at the gateway post, he never grabbed a glove to take the field in crimson flannels. RBI single, plus an extra base for the year.

8 In the sixth frame of a game against the A's on September 24, 1940, the Sox became the first team in AL history to blast four home runs in a single inning. The four came off the bats of the club's first baseman, shortstop, third baseman, and left fielder. Name all for a four-bagger, single for only three.

9 What Crimson Hose great has long held the AL record for the most pinch homers in a season with five? Single, plus two RBI for his record year.

10 On June 18, 1953, in the seventh inning of a game against the Tigers, Red Sox gardener Gene Stephens accomplished something in that frame that had never before been done by an AL player. What was it? RBI double.

11 On June 10, 1953, a certain right fielder became the first BoSoxer to stroke six hits in a single game. Better known for his glove than his bat, he hit .272 that year with a rather lowly .683 OPS. Triple.

12 The AL record for the fewest hits allowed in two consecutive complete games belongs to a Boston hurler, who surrendered just one hit in the two contests. Think about this a moment, and many of you will come up with the obvious answer. Others who are unaware of this one-of-a-kind AL feat need to do their homework on Sox no-hit hurlers. Two-bagger.

13 What BoSoxer was the most recent AL pitcher to crack two homers in one game? During his career, this righty pumped 12 seat-reachers, with half of them coming in that special season for Kasko's crew. RBI double.

14 The Tigers' Frank Lary was nicknamed "the Yankee Killer," but in 1954 a certain Boston chucker outdid even Lary as he slaughtered the Bombers, going 4–0 against them en route to an otherwise mediocre 11–12 slate. Twice a 12-game winner during the 1950s, he closed his nine-year career after 1958 with a 69–72 record, exclusively with Crimson Hose teams that never once finished ahead of the Yanks. Two-run double.

AB: 14
Hits: 14
Total Bases: 29
RBI: 17

INNING 7
MEMORABLE MONIKERS

We're not so kind as to ask you who was called "the Splendid Splinter." But several of the nicknames in this category are nearly as famous in Sox lore. And, of course, there are some designed to separate the men from the boys.

1 The Gray Eagle. Single.

2 Pudge. Cinch single.

3 Boob. RBI double.

4 The Monster. RBI single.

5 Dizzy. RBI double.

6 Boo. One-run single.

7 The Gerbil. Single.

8 Tilly. RBI double.

9 Pinch. Two-run homer.

10 Boomer. Two answers possible so take a single for each.

11 Skeeter. Triple.

12 El Guapo. RBI single.

13 Riverboat. Solo homer.

14 Psycho. RBI single.

15 The Golden Greek. RBI single.

AB: 15
Hits: 15
Total Bases: 27
RBI: 11

INNING 8
FORGOTTEN UNFORGETTABLES

1 In 1962 he manned right field in Fenway and slugged 18 homers in 398 at bats while hitting .294. He then whacked 22 seat-reachers the following year, but alas, those were his highlights, as his career quickly tanked. Still, there are those who can still envision him leaping fruitlessly for the ball Maris belted for number 61. Two-bagger.

2 In addition to Tony C., several other teenagers debuted with the Sox in the 1960s, and this performer was one of them. At age 23, he joined Yaz as Boston's All-Star reps in 1970, but after that it was all downhill as he floated to six other clubs over the next five seasons and was never again more than a reserve receiver. Part the Charles River with a RBI double.

3 His .310 batting mark in 101 games in 1945 might have won the AL hitting crown according to the rules then in vogue, as he played 100 or more games and had a higher BA than Snuffy Stirnweiss, who was awarded the title instead with a .309 figure. It was his lone season as a BoSox regular, and he was gone after rapping .138 in 1946, mostly as a pinch hitter. Solo homer for the name of this stocky right fielder who swung from the left side.

4 Who was the only Sox southpaw to fan 100 batters twice during the 1990s? Released by the Braves after toiling with the Expos, he went 12–4 as a starter-reliever during his first full season at Fenway and stayed in Beantown, mostly ineffectively, for the next three years. Tough double.

5 His entire seven-year career was spent with the Sox. After his first three seasons, he owned a .354 lifetime BA, just two points shy of Ted Williams at the same juncture. He played on three Boston flag winners, knocked only one career home run—that in 1914—and slid to a career .269 BA after slapping just .215 in his last four seasons, capped by an abysmal 1-for-12 finale in 1917, all 12 AB coming as a pinch hitter. Name him for a homer.

6 Somehow this hot-corner man was the Sox' lone All-Star representative for two straight seasons, hitting .279 and .282, respectively, before drifting into oblivion by age 29. Recoup your losses thus far and stop at second.

7 A backup in 1905, his rookie year, he became the Sox' frontline receiver by default in 1906 when Lou Criger missed most of the year and two yearling backstoppers, Bill Carrigan and Bob Peterson, were too green for full-time duty. In 72 games he crushed the pill for a .144 BA, an all-time BoSox season low among players with a minimum of 200 AB. You need to come armed with some heavy knowledge of early Sox lore to smack a grand-slam homer here.

8 One season he made just 17 hits in 104 games but nevertheless batted a respectable .270. The following year he slipped to .266 despite making 46 hits in 120 games. In his rookie season he shared the Boston clubhouse with a veteran infielder who had the same last name taped above his locker as our man did. RBI double, plus an extra ribby for the vet's full name.

9 A mound mainstay with the Sox ever since 1935, he seemingly reached his nadir in 1940 when he was tagged for 17 homers in just 157⅔ innings, coughed up 87 walks, and logged a dismal 5.08 ERA. Yet he achieved a snazzy .667 winning percentage when he went 12–6 as a combination starter-reliever to set a club record for the highest winning percentage by a qualifier with an ERA above 5.00. Three-bagger for the righty who notched a personal high 16 wins for the 1937 Sox.

10 No hurler in Boston AL history has ever gone winless for an entire season while working a minimum of 100 innings. What rookie came the closest in 1926 when he was 0–5 in 98 frames with a very respectable 3.58 ERA on a very unrespectable BoSox cellar entry? He left Boston early in the 1932 campaign with a 41–81 career log that improved sharply when he went 12–6 the following year and led the AL in saves with the loop flag winner. Double for him, RBI for his team in 1933.

11 As a rookie he led all Boston regulars in both BA and OPS. His sophomore season he slipped a tad to .330 but once again paced Sox regulars in BA and OPS. He spent the following season in the minors, never played another game for a Beantown entry, and finished with a .321 career BA in just 356 big-top games. But we haven't forgotten him, nor should you. Clues are there for a standup triple.

12 His team-leading four shutouts in 1973 were the most by a Sox southpaw since Parnell's glory days. Sounds like the Spaceman, does it? Remembering this inning's theme should steer you clear of Lee and onto this Newton, Mass., chucker. Double.

13 Who was the first African-American player the Sox acquired by trade? Gene Stephens went to Baltimore for the new man, who proceeded to flank Teddy Ballgame in center and also became the first player of color to appear regularly (105 games) in the BoSox lineup. RBI double.

14 Remember the 1990s cat who went nuts as a BoSox freshman, stroking .338 in 68 at bats with a whopping 1.026 OPS, only to crash to .218 with a .616 OPS in 79 at bats his soph season? Fleeing to Japan the following year, he led the Central League with 38 homers. Even die-hard Sox fans may get hosed here, so we'll go for three.

AB: 14
Hits: 14
Total Bases: 37
RBI: 11

INNING 9
RBI RULERS

1 Who paced the AL in RBI and copped the loop's Comeback Player of the Year honor during his only season as a BoSox regular? Interestingly, he failed to drive in a single run that April. Adding that he saw Series action with the Sox the previous year downgrades this to a double.

2 In the lone year he led the AL in RBI wearing Crimson Hose, he set the club all-time season ribby record. He's only a single, but his record number goes for two RBI.

3 Who was the most recent Red Soxer to collect 100 RBI during a season in which he fanned fewer than 30 times? He's also the most recent performer to achieve that feat with the Cubs. During his lengthy career, this consummate contact stickman never whiffed as many as 40 times. Single.

4 What Sox slugger nailed 137, 159, and 144 RBI, respectively, in three consecutive seasons but never won an AL RBI title outright while with Boston? Double.

5 In 1946 the Sox had the second, third, and fourth top RBI men in the AL. Name them in order and score a triple; down to a single if you know all three but not their order of finish; zip for anything less.

6 Who was the first switch-hitter to pace the Red Sox in RBI? He later drove in 100 while in the NL. Single, plus a RBI for the year he led Beantown.

7 Two years after setting an all-time club season record for runs, the Red Sox were led in RBI by a performer with the paltry total of 67. What year did this happen, and who was the team leader? Need both to triple here.

8 Between 1920 and Jimmie Foxx's arrival in 1936, who was the only Soxer to have a season in which he had as many as 10 homers and 100 RBI? Two bags for him, plus two RBI for his big year in Boston.

9 Excluding first basemen, who was the first rookie infielder (under the current freshmen qualifying rules) in Red Sox history to notch as many as 100 RBI? Two bags for him, one more for his year.

10 Strike years excepted, who posted the lowest season RBI total by a Sox team leader since expansion? He plated just 74 in 138 games after posting 71 and 70 in each of his two previous Fenway campaigns. Double, plus a RBI for his leadership year.

11 In Ted Williams's final season, he led the Sox in homers with 29 despite collecting just 310 AB. Who led the club in RBI that year with 103? Two-run double.

12 Three Sox sluggers have paced the AL in RBI in back-to-back seasons. Homer for all three, double for two, and a single for just one.

13 Prior to AL expansion in 1961, who was the only catcher among the Red Sox top 20 in career RBI? Double.

14 Between 1985 and 2004 only one Hub clouter topped the AL in ribbies, and he had to share the honor with a Cleveland clouter. Name both sluggers for a double, single for just one, plus a RBI for the year.

AB: 14
Hits: 14
Total Bases: 30
RBI: 10

GAME 3

INNING 1
SHELL-SHOCKED SLINGERS

1 Bet any member of the Red Sox faithful that he or she can't identify the BoSoxer that logged the club's highest season ERA to date while working as many as 100 innings and you'll rake in greenbacks by the bushel. After your patsy has guessed every execrable Sox hurler in creation, you might casually mention that our mystery man is a Hall of Famer. No joke. Even with that clue, we're wagering a triple, plus an extra base and a RBI for the year.

2 He truly befouled Beantown, posting the worst ERA (5.90) among ML qualifiers in 1964 and also the highest *ever* by a Sox qualifier. Three years later, Boston forced a seventh game against the Cards after sticking him with the loss in Game 6 of the 1967 World Series. Triple.

3 His .289 career winning percentage (39–96) with the Sox is the lowest among all hurlers who have worked a minimum of 1,000 innings in crimson hosiery. Need we add that he's in the Hall of Fame? RBI double.

4 At 23, he was a NL 18-game winner with a 2.94 ERA. At 28, he was a 10-game winner with an ERA over 5.00 in Sox garb. Among the top young lefties early in his career, he never started another game after turning 30. Single, plus a RBI for his appalling BoSox season.

5 Nine different BoSox slab men have suffered 20-loss seasons. Who is the only one of the nine to put up fewer than five victories to go with all those defeats? Homer for him, plus an extra RBI if you know his exact number of wins in his big loss season.

6 After a sterling rookie season, this former Bonus Baby's career nosedived as he posted the highest ERA (4.95) among AL qualifiers before being shipped to the Bucs in the Dick Stuart swap. RBI single.

7 Who is the only hurler to lose 20 or more games in a season twice while wearing Crimson Hose? Double for him, two RBI if you also know his big loss seasons.

8 Ten years after notching a 20-win campaign in the NL, he became the first Sox chucker ever to start over 25 games in a season in which he failed to average at least five innings per start. True, when your ERA exceeds 6.00, it's hard for any skipper to stomach your work for long. Double, plus a RBI for the year this flinger made 27 starts and worked only 127⅔ innings.

9 What year did the Sox have four pitchers who each lost 18 or more games? The year brings a double, the four hurlers an extra two bases, plus a RBI—but you need all four to score here.

10 The dubious honor of being the last pitcher to date to lose 20 games in a season wearing Red Sox raiment is shared by two men. The year the Sox faithful suffered through it rates two bases; the two big losers that season earn an extra base apiece, plus a RBI.

11 While leading the ML in hits surrendered, he became the only Sox lefty to shell out 300+ safeties in a season. He's also the last BoSox twirler to do so, regardless of arm persuasion, and as the game now is played, no one in Beantown is likely ever again to challenge him. Single, plus a RBI for the year.

12 What hurler won 10 games for the last-place Sox in 1927 despite allowing 11.34 hits per nine innings, the most ever surrendered by a BoSox lefty ERA qualifier? That same season he set a Crimson Hose record for the most losses by a southpaw with 18. Three-run homer.

13 No BoSox ERA qualifier allowed as many as 10 hits per nine innings prior to the end of the Deadball Era in 1919. Who came the closest when he permitted 9.63 hits per nine frames in 1911?

Knowing that it is not the only black mark currently beside his name should get you in for a double.

14 Only three Sox ERA qualifiers had seasons prior to expansion when they allowed as many as five walks per game. All had career-long control problems. Which of the trio did it as a rookie in 1954 when he logged 95 walks and just 69 strikeouts but nevertheless finished with a winning record (10–9) on a sub-.500 team? RBI triple for the first Sox hurler with at least 1,500 innings pitched to post a 4.00+ career ERA.

15 What longtime BoSox hill mainstay had a year from hell in his next-to-last season when he was tagged for 12 home runs in 46 innings and finished with a 7.83 ERA? His 2–3 mark that year exactly matched his won–lost figures as a rook in 1947. Use the clues to rack up a RBI double, plus an extra base for his year from Hades.

AB: 15
Hits: 15
Total Bases: 39
RBI: 16

INNING 2
HOME RUN KINGS

1 What Red Sox performer holds the AL record for the most seasons with at least 10 homers? Single, plus an extra base for the number of campaigns he reached double digits.

2 Just once in over 10 years in Red Sox threads did he top the club in four-baggers, and it occurred when he slammed 21, a personal best. Although he never donned pinstripes, he holds the Sox career homer mark among players born in the Bronx. Double.

3 A certain Sox slugger pounded a career-high 40 homers one season to set the AL record (later broken) for dingers at his position. Work out his position and he's yours for a single, plus a RBI for the year.

4 What Red Sox first sacker who smote just two circuit clouts in his five-year ML career was the first batter ever to jack one over the leftfield barrier in Fenway? This one is too well known to trivia buffs for us to ante up more than a double.

5 After hitting just five home runs in two seasons as a regular with the Sox, what outfielder tied for the AL home run crown with Babe Ruth the year after he left Boston? RBI triple.

6 The BoSox slugger who set the season record for dingers by a DH and then broke his own mark the following year is worth no more than a charitable single.

7 The only man to hit as many as 100 jacks while serving at third base for the Sox is Frank Malzone. Whose club third-base career-homer mark did he break? RBI double.

8 Since the late 1930s, only one BoSox outfielder with a minimum of 400 PA has gone an entire season without homering. Dealt to the Rangers during the offseason, he really showed his stuff, posting over 650 PA without going deep even once. In 5,000+ career at bats, this punchless pastureman hit just 11 taters. Double, plus a RBI for his lone Sox season.

9 Whose club career record for a performer who saw action principally in center field did Reggie Smith break when he hit his 88th dinger for the Sox? May prove tougher for many of you than it looks to us, so we'll go for two.

10 Prior to AL expansion in 1961, Ted Williams ranked first and Jackie Jensen second in the most career home runs by a Sox gardener. Who was third? Three-bagger.

11 Tall for a catcher at 6'4", he blasted 14 dingers as a rook and 17 more two years hence. The latter figure remained tops among BoSox backstops until Fisk eclipsed him eight years later. Two for this towering Tennessean.

12 Who is the only Soxer to blast 40 or more homers in a season on three occasions while fanning fewer than 100 times in each campaign? Single.

13 Prior to 1920, the onset of the Lively Ball Era, five men who totaled at least 400 career at bats with the Sox averaged at least one home run in every 100 AB while with Boston. Name all five for a hard-earned grand slam. Triple if you know only four. Single for three.

14 Who was the first Sox lefty swinger to power over 25 homers for six straight years? Learning that he did not play exclusively with the BoSox eliminates Ted Williams and should lead you to another clubber's door. Single.

AB: 14
Hits: 14
Total Bases: 28
RBI: 8

INNING 3
MASTER MOUNDSMEN

1 During the BoSox AL-record 15-year skein (1919–1933) in which they finished below .500 in every season, who among all hurlers on the club in a minimum of 500 innings during that span was the only one to post a winning percentage above .500? He went 54–52 for a .509 mark with the Sox. Double.

2 In that same 15-year skein, only two other hurlers won as many as 50 games in Sox array. One was a staff bulwark a few years into the skein, the other a linchpin toward the end of it. Get both and salt away a home run. Single for just one.

3 One more poser about that awful stretch in Sox history. What 200-game winner who totaled over 800 innings in Boston garb during that 15-year span became the first man in history to lose at least 50 career games with both the Red Sox and the Yankees? Double.

4 What hurler posted seven shutouts but nonetheless went only 15–15 for a Sox flag winner? It was his first year in Sox raiment, and two years earlier he had bagged eight shutouts while again winning just 15 games, this time with the last-place A's. Plenty of clues to score a triple here.

5 Precisely 10 men have won 100 or more games in Sox garb. Who are the only two of the 10 never to pitch for another ML team? You really need to know your Sox hill history to nail this one, so we'll treat correct responders to a solo homer but only if you get both men.

6 You'll win many a wager by asking Boston fans to name the only other pitcher besides Roger Clemens to lead the club outright in victories between 1986 and 1994. Set your sites on this vet who went 15–11 at age 37 with a sub-.500 crimson crew. It's always survival of the fittest in our books, so we'll go for three.

7 Name the four hurlers who won in double figures for the last Boston world champ prior to the 2004 squad. Three bases for all four, scratch single for knowing only three.

8 The first Boston AL flag winner featured three 20-game winners. They're worth a two-bagger, plus a RBI for knowing the 13-game winner who backed them up.

9 What Hub chucker once shared the AL lead in wins when he collected 18 victories in his sophomore season? Three for him, one more base for his big season.

10 Who was the only BoSox tosser to post a 20-win season in the decade of the 1950s? Two bases, plus a RBI for his 20-win year.

11 Numerous Sox hurlers have lost 20 or more games for last-place teams. Who is the only one to *win* 20 games for a cellar finisher? Nab a double here, plus an extra base for his big year.

12 What Sox hurler pitched on a first-division team that finished above .500 but nevertheless registered a sub-.500 winning percentage (12–13) despite logging a microscopic 1.69 ERA? Double for him, RBI for his extraordinarily unlucky year.

13 What pitcher's career line reads 96–54 with a .640 winning percentage in 1,375⅔ innings and a 2.94 ERA, all of it with the Red Sox? Experts will snatch up those numbers and sprint to a triple.

AB: 13
Hits: 13
Total Bases: 34
RBI: 5

INNING 4
NO-HIT NUGGETS

1 The first Boston Americans no-no was a classic, nothing less than a perfect game. Nail the year it happened, the Boston hurler who perpetrated it, and his mound opponent to nab a triple. Single if you only know the Hub hurler and year.

2 The first chucker to throw a no-no for a Boston World Series participant achieved the honor only about two and a half months before a teammate matched his feat. Name him for a double, plus an extra base for his no-hit teammate and a RBI for the year.

3 This Red Sox ace was not only the first African American to pitch a no-no in the AL but also the most recent junior-circuit twirler to homer while holding the opposition hitless. RBI single, plus an extra base for the year.

4 Who was the first Sox hurler to notch two no-nos while in Beantown? Double, plus two RBI if you know the two years he did it.

5 What Red Sox hurler was credited with a perfect game for many years even though he faced only 26 batters? He's worth a single, plus two RBI if you know the circumstances that caused him to face only 26 sticks.

6 It's rare indeed to hold the opposition hitless and still lose, but that's just what this luckless lefty Soxer did when Cleveland handed him a 2–1 road loss in which he hurled only eight innings. Demoted to the pen by May, he failed to win any games that year before moving to the Tribe himself the following campaign. RBI single for him, plus an extra base for his ill-fated year.

7 What Sox righty was deprived only by a controversial scorer's decision from throwing two consecutive no-hitters in 1923? His no-no came against the team he later pitched for in a World Series. Two bases for him, one for his team to be.

8 When Mel Parnell no-no'd the White Sox on July 14, 1956, and in the process perpetrated the lone no-hitter to date in which the no-no hurler made the final putout, how many years had it been since a Red Sox hurler last fashioned a no-hitter? RBI triple.

9 What Sox backstop caught three no-hitters despite playing 100 games in a season just once in his 10-year career, all of it served in Boston gear? Interestingly, the last two came in his coda season when he caught just 27 contests. Triple.

10 Who was the youngest pitcher ever to toss a no-hitter in Red Sox livery? Double.

11 Two years after leading the AL in saves with 42, this 6'6" sinkerballer fashioned the only no-hitter in the majors, baffling the Devil Rays during a 10–0 rout at Fenway. Single, plus a RBI for the year.

12 He exited the majors with a weak 40–64 career record, but at age 23 he spun what proved to be the last Sox no-no for 36 years in defeating the Indians 2–0 before a paid crowd of just 1,247. Take three bases for him and a RBI for naming the opposing Tribe moundsman who later starred with Boston.

13 In his first game in BoSox garb he held Baltimore hitless, but a 13–10 record and a 4.50 ERA made him expendable after just one season in the Hub. Single for him, plus a RBI for his lone year with the Sox.

14 Early Wynn took the loss when this Medford, Mass., moundsman defeated the White Sox 1–0 at Comiskey Park. Take a single for him, a RBI for the year of his no-no, and an extra base for the BoSox catcher who scored the game's lone run.

15 For a bunt single, which Soxer tossed a no-hitter in his second big league game?

AB: 15
Hits: 15
Total Bases: 32
RBI: 12

INNING 5
WHAT WAS THEIR REAL HANDLE?

1 Trot Nixon. Double.

2 Rudy York. Three bases.

3 Nomar Garciaparra. RBI single.

4 Tex Hughson. Double.

5 Tex Clevenger. Triple.

6 Catfish Metkovich. Solo homer.

7 Spike Owen. Double.

8 Duffy Lewis. Triple.

9 Reggie Smith. RBI single.

10 J. D. Drew. RBI double.

11 Oil Can Boyd. RBI single.

12 Jake Stahl. Two-run triple.

13 Sparky Lyle. RBI single.

14 Lefty Grove. RBI single.

15 Smokey Joe Wood. Three-run homer.

AB: 15
Hits: 15
Total Bases: 33
RBI: 12

INNING 6
CIRCLING THE GLOBE

1 The first Dominican-born Sox pitcher went 5–1 in his only season at Fenway before moving to the Dodgers but had previously fared far better elsewhere. We can't offer more than a bloop single, plus a RBI for the year.

2 This hurler owns a lot of Boston AL firsts, including being the club's initial performer born in Wales. Later a college prexy, he began his career with the NL Boston entry in the late 1890s. Two-run double.

3 The first native of Mexico to work at least 50 games in a season did it with the Red Sox in 1969. In his two-year Fenway stint, he logged exactly 100 appearances, mostly as a reliever, and notched 17 saves. Double.

4 This gardener's 496 at bats with the red-hosed entry in 1907 remain the club's season record for a player born in Canada. He came to Boston from Cleveland, and that's no bull. Two-run homer.

5 El Tiante was *grande* in Boston, but a Havana-born hurler who preceded Luis in the Hub by some 20 years actually holds the club's record for career games pitched by a native Cuban. In parts of seven seasons he appeared in 286 contests with the Sox, mostly from the pen. RBI double.

6 Like many ML clubs in the 1920s, the BoSox tried a Cuban import. An infielder, he stood only 5'6" and his power numbers reflected his small size. He was around only for 1925 and 1926, never saw regular duty, and hence rates a grand slam and our deep admiration.

7 This performer, who died in Milwaukee where he lived for most of his life, was 25–26 for the 1926–1927 Sox and remains to this day the club's most notable player who was born in Deutschland. Two-run homer.

8 The only BoSox player to date who was born in Scotland clubbed the last five of his 264 career homers with Boston as a teammate of Ted. They were also the only five dingers he hit as an ALer. Two bags for this famous NL fall hero.

9 The first hurler born in Canada to win as many as 20 career games for the Sox was a lefty whose bat was nearly as solid as his arm. He rapped .316 for the 1946 Phils after being named to the AL All-Star squad three years earlier while with the Sox. Two-run homer.

10 You're a winner for recalling the Dutch chucker who appeared in 22 games for the Red Sox between 1979 and 1980. We're wagering a solo shot that this Netherlands righty has slipped into the nether regions of your memory.

11 Daisuke Matsuzaka made headlines after signing his lucrative contract with the Sox, but Boston's first Japanese-born player appeared with far less fanfare and made 25 starts in parts of three Beantown seasons. Single, plus a RBI for his debut year.

12 Prior to Manny Ramirez, who held the BoSox mark for career games played by a native of the Dominican Republic? An 18-year vet, he spent four seasons in Boston, playing over 100 games each campaign. A five-time All-Star in the NL, he finished there in 1997. Single.

13 Mexico furnished the Red Sox with their first-string center fielder in 1935. A left-handed hitter with good speed, he later starred with Washington and the Browns before finishing with the 1939 Dodgers. Two-run triple.

14 Who is the only Canadian hurler to start a World Series game for the Sox? Adding that his surname matches that of a current big league city makes this worth just one.

AB: 14
Hits: 14
Total Bases: 35
RBI: 18

INNING 7
STELLAR STICKWIELDERS

1 In his final ML season (minimum 500 PA) he led Boston's first AL cellar dweller in BA, OBP, SA, OPS, home runs, RBI, games played, and walks. His name will bring a double, and the reason that season proved to be his finale is worth a RBI.

2 For an easy single, who set the current season record for the most doubles in Red Sox garb? Take a RBI for his total and another for the year he did it.

3 What Sox middle infielder once led the AL in doubles with 51 after having previously won an AL doubles crown with another club? Two bases.

4 In the five-year span between 1954 and 1958 only one ALer totaled as many as 40 doubles in a season, and he played for Boston. Name him for a two-bagger, plus a ribby for the year he led the AL with 40 two-basers.

5 Who was the only hitsmith to rip 50 two-baggers in a season twice as a member of the Sox? The second time he reached the half-century mark, he tied for the AL lead, belting the highest doubles total seen in Boston in over 70 years. Single.

6 After stroking .347 with 19 homers in 386 at bats, this switch-hitter led all Sox batting-title qualifiers at .319 the following year. Reduced to a part-timer the next two seasons, he briefly tried Japan before calling it quits. Used mostly as a DH with Boston, he also played the outfield and first base. RBI single.

7 What two Sox stars shared the AL triples crown one year with Washington shortstop Joe Cassidy? Their total of 19 fell only one short of the club record at that time. You'll fall short of a triple and end with zip if you don't know both men, plus a RBI for the year they tied.

8 The Sox club record holder for the most triples in a season failed to lead the AL in three-baggers the year he set the mark with 22. He's worth a double, and his record-setting year rates a RBI.

9 When Dom DiMaggio and Bobby Doerr tied with Detroit's Hoot Evers for the AL lead in triples in 1950 with a modest total of 11, how many years had it been since a Crimson Hoser had attained even so much as a share of the AL three-bagger crown? You must come within two years to score a triple of your own.

10 Who won an AL bat crown in Sox garb three years after posting a .608 OPS with another AL outfit, the lowest of any junior-loop bat-title qualifier that season? Two bases for him, plus a ribby for his weak OPS campaign.

11 What Hall of Famer was the first Soxer to play at least 130 games in a year in which he turned 39 or older? We'll add that he fanned just 33 times in 561 plate appearances and still award a headfirst double, plus a RBI for the year.

12 The first Soxer age 40 or older to play in at least half his team's games hit Beantown in 1935 and rapped .304 in 78 contests while leading the AL in pinch hits before leaving the bigs a year later. A regular pastureman on the dynastic A's from 1929–1931, this Iowan's given name was Edmund, but everyone called him by his nickname. Triple.

13 Wes Ferrell, with .308, leads all pitchers who amassed a minimum of 100 career at bats with the Red Sox. If you know the first hurler in club history who can claim a .300 career BA with at least 100 career AB in a Boston AL uniform, treat yourself to a three-run homer.

14 Who was the first Sox batting-title qualifier to post a 1.000+ OPS in a season while hitting below .300? He had almost done it the previous year by striking .300 even, with a 1.001 OPS. Single.

15 Prior to Manny Ramirez's arrival, who had posted the Sox highest season SA by a batting-title qualifier since the days of Ted Williams? That year this performer batted .333 and slugged a league-leading .637 in his penultimate season in Beantown before inking a big free-agent deal elsewhere. Single, plus a RBI for the year.

AB: 15
Hits: 15
Total Bases: 30
RBI: 13

INNING 8
RBI RULERS

1 Among players who collected a minimum of 3,000 career at bats with the Red Sox, what gardener holds the record for the fewest RBI with 270? He also managed just one home run in his years in Fenway. Triple.

2 Who held the Sox career mark for RBI by a third sacker prior to AL expansion in 1961? Double.

3 What BoSox clubber posted the lowest season BA in ML history by a 100-RBI performer? In addition, he rarely walked, netting just 29 free passes in over 600 plate appearances as he logged the lowest season OBP ever (.254) by a 30-homer man. Single for this one-dimensional slugger, a RBI for the year, plus an extra base for knowing his lowly BA.

4 Who broke Cy Young's club record for the most career RBI by a Red Sox pitcher when he bagged his 82nd and final ribby in Sox garb? Unlike Young, some of his ribbies came as a pinch hitter. RBI single.

5 What slugger collected 101 career homers for the team from Fenway but had only 377 RBI? Two-run double.

6 The Sox have had a bevy of shortstops that knocked home 100+ runs. However, they had a lengthy drought between Rico Petrocelli's 1970 campaign and the next BoSox shortstop to hit the century mark. Who was he? RBI single.

7 What first sacker collected 2,006 at bats with the Red Sox but tagged just three home runs and accounted for only 261 RBI? Born in Gloucester, Mass., and exiting in Ipswich, he'd had a 100 RBI season with another AL team earlier in his career. Two-run double.

8 Six times in his career, Ted Williams posted 25 or more home runs in a season with fewer than 100 RBI. Who was the only other Soxer prior to AL expansion in 1961 to have even one such season? Solo homer.

9 The player who broke Pinky Higgins's Sox season mark for ribbies by a hot-corner denizen retired with fewer than 400 career RBI. Single.

10 Prior to 1950, when Ted Williams had 97 RBI and just 334 at bats, who held the club record for most RBI with fewer than 400 AB (the standard in 1950 for a bat-title qualifier)? We'll tell you he set the mark in 1920 with 73 RBI in 363 AB and still award a three-run homer.

11 What year did Boston win the AL pennant with a shortstop leading all veteran players on the club with a mere 62 ribbies? Tricky single, plus an extra base for the shortstop in question.

12 He played only two years with the BoSox, but in his first Sox campaign he topped the AL with 118 RBI and then paced the Sox with 114 the following year, just four behind the junior-loop leader. Careful or this slugger may slip through your fingers like many of the balls hit his way. RBI single.

13 The Sox all-time record for the most RBI in a season with fewer than 10 home runs belongs to the older brother of a man who later led the Sox in RBI in each of his last two seasons in the majors. The elder brother posted 119 ribbies despite going deep just seven times while the younger sib finished his career in 1945. Last but far from least—both sibs also took turns leading the Sox in home runs. Can you nail these two brothers for a two-run double?

14 Prior to Carlton Fisk's huge year in 1977, only one catcher in Red Sox history had put together a season in which he hit .300, scored at least 50 runs, and totaled at least 60 RBI. Name him for a double.

AB: 14
Hits: 14
Total Bases: 29
RBI: 15

INNING 9
RED-HOT ROOKIES

1 Which of the following Red Sox rookie records is the only one that does not currently belong to Ted Williams? SA, OBP, runs, RBI, total bases, walks, home runs. RBI single.

2 What future AL bat champ was the only rookie to collect so much as one at bat for the 1903 World Champion Boston Americans? Double.

3 Bonus Babies who fashioned 10-year careers in the majors were few in the 1950s. What big-bucks yearling broke in with Boston in 1953 at age 18 with a .215 BA in 47 games and lasted until 1962 despite posting a career .221 BA in just 603 games? Worth a triple.

4 The Sox record holder for the highest batting average by a rookie qualifier (400 at bats) will send all but the experts in search of an alibi if they don't triple here.

5 Acquired in the deal that sent fan-favorite Tony C. to the Angels, this slick fielder got his first real shot at the bigs with the 1971 Sox and topped AL rooks in hits and doubles while tying for the loop frosh lead in runs. Regardless, he was never much with the stick, retiring with a woeful .598 career OPS in over 2,000 at bats. Double.

6 In 1906 this Red Sox twirler led all AL rookies with 20 complete games. He also set an all-time record that Crimson Hose followers are loath to mention: the fewest wins by a hurler who completed 20 or more starts in a season. Name him for a three-bagger, plus a RBI for his win total.

7 After giving him brief looks over two campaigns, the Sox granted this Massachusetts-born lad his first real shot and he responded with an 11–8 slate plus three shutouts, the most by a BoSox freshman southpaw in nearly 60 years. Dealt just a year later, he concluded his 15-year big league sojourn in 1984. Double.

8 You're in for a cold time in this category if you don't know the Beantowner that led all AL rookies in 1901 with a 2.80 ERA. Two-run triple for this righty who collected all but one of his 83 career wins in Boston livery.

9 Loser of 17 games as a rook with a weak 4.48 ERA, more than a run higher than the league average, he emerged as the ace on a Sox flag winner just two years hence and retired with over 150 victories. Single, plus a RBI for his inauspicious debut year.

10 In 1908 the Sox tried this Vermont product at second, and he paced ML rookies in runs, batting, slugging, and OBP while stealing 31 sacks. After slipping offensively as a soph, he went to the Pale Hose during the 1910 season. Even our adding that he went by a diminutive form of his given name (Ambrose) still makes this a two-run triple.

11 His first full season came the year our previous frosh debuted, and this Maine native topped ML yearlings in hits and then paced the Sox with a .311 BA in 1909. Packaged with the preceding rook to the White Sox, this third sacker with the aristocratic surname is worth a solo homer.

12 The first BoSoxer to lead all ML rookies in home runs banged seven round-trippers in what would now be considered his official frosh season. In addition, he set the still-existing club record for the most steals by a yearling with 35. He's worth a double; his rook year will bring a RBI.

13 His real first name was Heber and he won 19 games as a Sox frosh in 1941 even though he turned 32 that year. We'll toss in the generous clue that the Sox had an infielder in 1941 with the same last name as his and still cough up a triple.

14 Which of the following early-day Boston AL stars did not make his ML debut with the Sox? Freddy Parent, Hobe Ferris, Joe Wood, Duffy Lewis, Tris Speaker, Ray Collins. Double.

15 In 1946 the Sox won the AL flag despite producing no rookies of consequence. Who was the club's only freshman to collect as many as 50 at bats or pitch as many as 25 innings? Born in Boston, he'll earn you a two-run homer.

AB: 15
Hits: 15
Total Bases: 38
RBI: 11

GAME 4

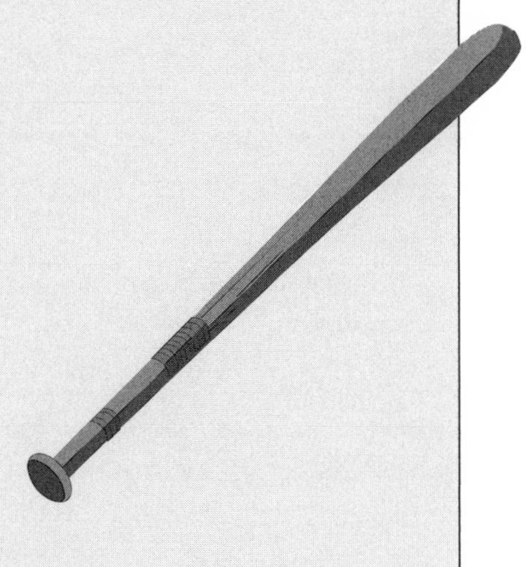

INNING 1
JACK OF ALL TRADES

1 He began his ML career as a shortstop with Washington, came to the Sox in 1958 as a second baseman, and left the Hub after five seasons as the first man in history to win batting crowns as both a second baseman and a first baseman. RBI single.

2 In parts of five seasons cobbled together over three separate stints with the BoSox, he saw action at every position, plus DH. During his lone Sox hill appearance, he finished a 14–1 loss against the Twins, working a scoreless inning and fanning Chuck Knoblauch. An outfielder for the most part, he's a RBI single.

3 To date, who is the only Red Sox performer to play all nine positions in one season? The Sox lost 100+ games in each of his first three campaigns in crimson hosiery and finished last in all but one of the eight years he was with the club. Usually found in the pasture, he can be jacked out for a homer, plus an added RBI for the year he played everywhere.

4 Although a fixture at third base for most of his career, Wade Boggs actually played more games at another spot as a rookie. Peg that position for a single.

5 Billy Goodman played more than 35 games at five different positions during his lengthy career with the Sox. Name all five for a three-bagger. Single for four.

6 A Sox regular at third and short, he once led the AL with 47 doubles, cranking over 20 apiece that year playing both second and third. His coda season came in the NL, where he saw action at all four infield positions. RBI single.

7 Two years after debuting in center field with the Sox, this lefty made 28 appearances from their pen and then 29 more the following season. Few players since expansion have made this switch either way, so he's one of the rare recent "jacks of all trades." Double.

8 He broke in as a pitcher in a major league that no longer exists and was the first performer to be a Sox regular at two different positions: first base and right field. Home run.

9 This versatile glove man played at least 20 games at three different infield positions for a Sox flag winner and then started four contests in that year's World Series solely at second. On a dare that you don't know your Sox middle infielders, we'll ante up a RBI single.

10 In his three seasons with the Sox in the mid-1930s, he played all four infield positions and was a regular during his career at each of them except first base. Dropped by the Sox after hitting just .156 in 46 games in 1938, he rebounded the following year to rap .324 for the Pale Hose. Triple.

11 Buddy Myer broke in as a shortstop and finished as a second baseman. What position did he play during his lone full season with the Red Sox? Single, plus a RBI for the year in question.

12 Employed at five different positions in his 265 career games in Sox threads, he played three games as a late-inning defensive replacement for Spike Owen in the 1986 Fall Classic. The pride of Santurce, Puerto Rico, he's good for a RBI single.

13 In 1914, his lone year as bat qualifier, he played 145 games and saw action at each infield position in at least six games, with second base his high with 59 appearances. He played 10 years in the majors and was on two Sox flag winners. RBI triple for this consummate utilityman who was born in Haverhill, Mass., and died in Boston.

14 The exact antithesis of a "jack of all trades," he's the only man to appear in as many as 1,500 games in Sox garb and play only one position during his entire Hub career. After we also note that he holds the ML records for the most games at his position without playing elsewhere, and the most contests played solely at one position while performing exclusively for one ML team, he goes for only a single.

AB: 14
Hits: 14
Total Bases: 27
RBI: 10

INNING 2
HOME RUN KINGS

1 Earl Wilson owns the BoSox record for the most career home runs by a pitcher, with 17, and Wes Ferrell is second with one less. The fifth spot on the list, with a modest total of six, is occupied by the only man to collect as many as 1,000 at bats with the Sox while serving as a moundsman. Name him for a RBI single.

2 Among performers who collected a minimum of 5,000 plate appearances with the Red Sox, who ranks last in career homers with just 14? Two-run triple.

3 What post-1920 player led the BoSox in taters one year but played fewer than 200 games in Sox threads? This South Carolina swinger creamed 35 for the club lead and exited early the next season. Single.

4 Who is the only outfielder with as many as 5,000 career plate appearances with the Sox to average less than one home run for every 100 at bats? Our clue that 45 of his 75 career jacks came with the ChiSox knocks this down to a RBI double.

5 The only man to wear a BoSox uniform for a minimum of five full seasons and bat less than .250 while hitting fewer than 10 home runs during his Hub days is going for a RBI triple these days.

6 Who belted the most career homers for the Sox without ever making an All-Star squad in crimson garb? He clubbed over 20 homers three straight seasons in Beantown and later stroked .357 for the BoSox in a World Series. RBI single.

7 The only BoSox performer prior to AL expansion in 1961 with a minimum of 1,500 plate appearances to average over three home runs per 100 at bats despite carrying a sub-.250 career BA while in Hub garb was an infielder. Name this fan favorite who was part of the 1952–1953 Sox youth movement but never once in his 10 ML seasons played enough to qualify for a bat title and snare a solo homer.

8 Five men with a minimum of 2,000 plate appearances with the Red Sox prior to AL expansion in 1961 averaged over four home runs per 100 at bats. Name all five for a three-run homer. Triple for four. Single for three.

9 The leader in career home runs among performers with fewer than 1,000 at bats in Boston AL garb tagged 40 for the Sox, with a high of 22 in 1951. His name rates a triple even after we tell you that in his big dinger season he set the present club record for the fewest extra base hits (33) by a 20-homer man.

10 Who is the only catcher to crack 20+ homers on a BoSox pennant winner? Ponder the identity of this Worcester, Mass., native and then dive for a headfirst double.

11 Who is the only man in Sox history to club 10 or more homers in a season in which he collected fewer than 100 at bats? Single for him, extra base for the year he did it.

12 The highest season SA in Sox history by a batsman who collected at least 502 plate appearances (enough to qualify for the bat title in any era) while failing to hit a single home run is .411. The owner of that mark posted a higher OBP (.416) than SA that season, and it proved to be his last in BoSox raiment. RBI double.

13 In 1945 the ball was dead and most of the game's top sluggers were in the armed services. Bob Johnson led the Red Sox with 12 homers. Who was second to Johnson with 11 dingers and topped the club with 81 runs and a .822 OPS? Hit this one in the drink for a homer and collect three RBI to go with it.

AB: 13
Hits: 13
Total Bases: 32
RBI: 14

INNING 3
TUMULTUOUS TRADES

Nothing else in Sox history rivals the Ruth deal, but that was a sale not a trade. The transactions we highlight here were all swaps that impacted greatly on the Sox future fortunes, both positively and negatively.

1 A future NL Rookie of the Year and the only man to toss a no-hitter that same season were dealt with two other players by the Sox. Name them for a single. Add an extra base for knowing the two main cogs Boston received in this swap.

2 What key member of the 1903 world champs was dealt to the New York AL entry on June 17, 1904, for Bob Unglaub, a rookie infielder that injuries prevented from fulfilling his early promise? RBI double.

3 After he saw only limited action in two seasons with the Sox, what future NL batting champ was given away with reliever Mike Gonzalez and cash for Jeff Suppan, plus two others? Single.

4 To acquire an aging Hall of Famer who had just one season left in his tank, following the 1904 season the Sox swapped a future AL bat king. Name both players involved in this Boston blunder and score a RBI double.

5 A rapidly fading Dick McAuliffe was all the Sox received in exchange for this future AL home run champ who would clout over 200 round-trippers in the next 13 seasons. Single.

6 What future Hall of Famer departed the Sox in a preseason 1916 deal for Sam Jones, Fred Thomas, and $55,000 that was nearly as devastating to the club's future fortunes as the Ruth transaction? Triple.

7 On June 3, 1952, the Sox swapped Johnny Pesky, Walt Dropo, and three lesser lights to Detroit for four Tigers stars in what appeared initially to be a Sox steal but didn't work out that way. Which of the following players was not involved in that blockbuster transaction? George Kell, Hoot Evers, Fred Hatfield, Don Lenhardt, Clyde Vollmer. Double.

8 Boston hated to give up Jimmy Piersall, but the Sox got two valuable regulars from Cleveland in exchange for him, one a slugging first sacker and the other a future centerfield replacement for Piersall. Nail both and score a triple. Single for just one.

9 What future Hall of Famer was gift wrapped to the Yankees on June 30, 1923, in exchange for Camp Skinner, George Murray, Norm McMillan, and 50 grand? Double.

10 Which of the following members of the 1919 Red Sox did not later join Ruth in the massive Hub exodus to the Yankees? Braggo Roth, Everett Scott, Mike McNally, Sad Sam Jones, Wally Schang, Harry Hooper. Double.

11 Ted Cox, Rick Wise, Mike Paxton, and Bo Diaz went to Cleveland in exchange for Fred Kendall and a certain hurler for what would be his first of two stints in Sox threads before his Cooperstown induction. Single for his name.

12 What future AL batting titlist accompanied Roy Johnson from the Tigers in a 1932 deal for Earl Webb that became one of the Sox' rare coups in that era? RBI single.

13 Name the Philadelphia A's hurler that came in the same package with Jimmie Foxx for a $150,000 slice of Tom Yawkey's fortune, plus Gordon Rhodes and minor league catcher George Savino and score a solo homer. A solid arm with the A's, he won in double figures only once with the Sox before moving on to the Browns in 1939.

14 Sox fans are forever haunted by the covenant GM Lou Gorman engineered late in 1990 to acquire a righty reliever for the stretch drive. So infamous is this straight-up swap that you'll need the bullpenner Boston received and the boy they squandered just to reach first base.

AB: 14
Hits: 14
Total Bases: 27
RBI: 4

INNING 4
TEAM TEASERS

1 What BoSox team holds the ML season record for slugging, total bases, and extra base hits? The Crimson Hose won 95 games under a skipper who exited the club after that season. Single for the year and a RBI for the pilot.

2 The lowest Sox team BA since the Deadball Era oddly enough came in a season when the Hub boasted the AL batting champ. Reason this strange year out for a clean single.

3 What post–Deadball Era Sox club had as its top three home run hitters Phil Todt, Ira Flagstead, and Wally Shaner, who combined to rap all of 13 taters? Home run.

4 In what year did the Sox score a team-record 1,027 runs? Easy RBI double for club experts who'll remember that it was also the most recent year the red hose rapped .300 as a unit.

5 During the Sox' first decade in existence (1901–1910), no one appeared in as many as 1,000 games with the club. In the 1971–1980 decade, however, a club-record four players appeared in 1,000 or more games with the Sox. Name all four and collect a single, plus two RBI. Sac fly RBI if you know only three.

6 What Sox team finished in the cellar just two years after winning the AL pennant? RBI single.

7 It's been a while since a Crimson Hose entry swiped 100+ sacks, but interestingly the Sox then proceeded to do it in consecutive seasons. Sounds like a Deadball Era effort, but actually the Babe had long since passed through Boston when these Hub units sported speed. Take a double for nailing the two-year run.

8 What Sox club had six pitchers make 12 or more starts, with five of them being the less than memorable Yank Terry, Clem Hausmann, Joe Bowman, Emmett O'Neill, and Pinky Woods? Two-run homer.

9 What was the most recent BoSox club to average at least one error per game? Just two years later, the red hose turned it around and won the pennant. RBI single.

10 The 1936 Red Sox finished sixth with a sub-.500 record but boasted five future Hall of Famers. Snag a well-deserved homer for the quintet, a double for four, zilch for anything less.

11 What was the only Sox club since the war years that failed to have a .300 hitter, a 20-homer stick, or a 100 RBI man? Injuries shelved the Sox' best bats that year as they went 73–89, placing last in the AL Eastern Division. RBI single.

12 Name the year the BoSox mound staff fanned a club record-low 310 hitters. Our clues are that Oscar Fuhr ranked fifth on the squad in hill Ks with just 27, and Tex Vache was the only hitter to whiff more than 30 times. Two-run homer.

13 What was the first Sox club to fan 1,000 batters in a season? A true team effort, as every major hurler fanned fewer than 180, it was also the first year that any AL club reached quadruple digits in Ks, with the Tribe also turning the trick. Knowing your history should help lead you to the year. Double.

14 The most recent Sox club that failed to capture a league flag despite boasting two 20-game winners is worth a single. But you can strive for two by nailing both members of this Hub hill tandem.

AB: 14
Hits: 14
Total Bases: 30
RBI: 13

INNING 5
MVP MARVELS

1 Originally the MVP honor was called the Chalmers Award and was given for the first time in 1911. Who led all BoSox players in Chalmers votes in 1911 and then won the award the following year? Single.

2 The AL began giving league MVP awards in 1922. What second sacker led all Sox players in the balloting that year, receiving seven votes? RBI triple.

3 In 1925, even though Boston finished deep in the AL cellar, a Sox gardener tied for seventh in the MVP balloting with 10 votes. You're entitled to wave your banner if you collect a solo homer on this toughie.

4 The final AL League MVP Award was given in 1928. What Sox infielder finished ninth with 11 votes? Two-run triple.

5 The present Baseball Writers' Association of America MVP awards were first given in 1931, and the Sox were blessed with the sixth-place finisher in that year's voting. Weave yourself a RBI double.

6 Wade Boggs never won a MVP Award, but he came closest while sporting Sox garb. In what year did Boggs finish highest in the balloting? Single, plus a RBI for knowing where he ranked in that season's voting.

7 The Twins' Cesar Tovar copped the only first-place vote that did not go to a certain Hub star the year he walked away with MVP honors. Grab a single, plus a RBI for his super season.

8 No Red Sox hurler before the expansion era snagged a MVP Award. Who came the closest when he finished second in 1935? Single.

9 The first Boston AL performer to win a BBWAA trophy was also the AL runner-up the following year. He's a single; the year goes for an extra base.

10 When Ted Williams won his first MVP Award in 1946, how many times had he previously finished second? Double, plus a RBI for each of his second-place finishes, if any.

11 Who was the first Red Sox position player born outside the U.S. to crack the top 10 in the MVP voting? In four Beantown seasons he belted 113 homers, but his inability to draw walks made him far less potent than meets the eye. Single for him, a RBI for the year he did well in the balloting, plus an extra base for his country of origin.

12 What Sox performer finished a surprising second in the 1950 MVP balloting, sandwiched between Yankees greats Rizzuto and Berra? Triple.

13 Who ranks as the youngest BoSoxer ever to notch a MVP vote? Mentioning that he was also the youngest AL regular in each of his first three seasons lowers this to a single, plus a RBI for the year he first copped a vote.

14 In 1960, Ted Williams's final season, he was only a part-time player. Who led all Soxers in the AL MVP balloting that year and what teammate finished just one rung behind him? Triple for both men, but you need to get them in the right order.

15 Who played the most career games in a Sox uniform without earning a single MVP vote of any kind? You can include the Chalmers, League, and Baseball Writers' honors and still come up with this outfielder that milled around for 1,101 games in crimson threads. He played on one BoSox pennant winner and missed appearing with another due to his retirement the previous year. Hard smash double.

AB: 15
Hits: 15
Total Bases: 31
RBI: 11

INNING 6
MOMENTS TO REMEMBER

1 On April 22, 2007, the Sox club experienced a Memorable Moment by blasting a record-tying four consecutive homers off Yankees frosh Chase Wright at Fenway. Triple for nailing this quartet, a single for three, zip for less.

2 What Red Sox swinger's Moment to Remember came when he set an all-time record by driving in all nine of the club's runs in a 10-inning victory? It was his 12th and last season, exclusively with Boston, but despite his nine RBI game, he totaled just 44 ribbies in 77 contests that year for Kevin Kennedy's crew. RBI single.

3 He bagged only 40 victories in his seven seasons with the Sox, but one of them was the club's first postseason win in 28 years. Name the southpaw whose Moment to Remember was a scoreless two-inning relief stint that helped earn him and the Sox a win in Game 1 of the 1946 World Series. Three-run triple.

4 The first documented player in AL history to homer on the initial pitch thrown to him in the bigs was a BoSoxer, and his Moment to Remember was sweetened because he was a pitcher. Alas, this lefty from Rhode Island never slammed another. Whack this one down the line for a bases-clearing triple, plus an extra sack and a RBI for the year.

5 Whose Moment to Remember came in the final game of the 1912 World Series when he scored the walk-off winning run on Larry Gardner's sacrifice fly? Two-run double.

6 Two Red Sox shortstops experienced Moments to Remember when they tied the post-1900 ML record by scoring six times in a regulation-length game. The pair turned the trick for BoSox pennant winners 40 years apart. Two bases, but you'll need both to score here.

7 He had not just one but two Moments to Remember when he scored the winning runs in both the first and last games of the 1918 World Series. Remarkably, they were the only two runs this infielder tallied in the six-game fray. Home run.

8 The first man to come to bat for Boston in an AL game never played for a Boston NL team yet collected his first major league at bat with a club that won a big league pennant representing Boston. His 1901 Moment to Remember occurred on April 26 in Boston's AL inaugural, a 10–6 win over Baltimore. RBI triple.

9 His Moment to Remember came in the lid-lifter of the 1946 World Series when he became the first BoSox performer to win a postseason game with an extra-inning home run after taking Howie Pollet deep in the 10th frame of a 3–2 triumph. The clue that he went homerless in postseason play the year before shaves this to a RBI two-bagger.

10 A certain player's performance for the Red Sox in a game on June 20, 1916, seemed unmemorable at the time, but it became a

Moment to Remember in 1920 when he played in his 578th consecutive ML game to break George Pinkney's old mark of 577. The streak continued until May 6, 1925, giving him a record string that lasted until it was surpassed later that year by a teammate of his named Gehrig. Double.

11 What BoSoxer's Moment to Remember came in the second game of a June 21 doubleheader against Detroit when he rang up his 12th consecutive hit in 12 at bats to set a record that has since been tied but never bettered? Double.

12 On April 14, 1967, this Red Sox frosh debuted brilliantly when he came within one strike of no-hitting the Yanks before Elston Howard singled cleanly. Boston fans savor this Moment to Remember, so we'll offer a double for the chucker, but an extra base, plus a RBI, for recalling his Fall River, Mass.-born catcher who also made his ML debut that day.

13 What BoSox pitcher's Moment to Remember came when he went behind the dish to catch both ends of a doubleheader at age 39 in 1942? Nearing 38 when he hit Boston in 1941, this reliever and spot starter nevertheless logged 183 games with the Sox over the next six seasons. RBI double.

14 The Sox tried him at first and behind the dish even though he stood 6'6", but in four seasons he couldn't hit a lick, poking only 18 hits in 120 career at bats for a measly .150 BA. However, this California lad's Moment to Remember occurred when he homered in his last career at bat, just two seasons after Ted Williams did so with just a bit more fanfare. Triple.

AB: 14
Hits: 14
Total Bases: 36
RBI: 12

INNING 7
PEERLESS PILOTS

1 Before 2007, who was the only Red Sox pilot to sit at the team's helm in more than one World Series? Double.

2 In 1903, Jimmy Collins became the first of his kind to manage a major league team in postseason play. What was his "kind"? Triple.

3 Who guided a BoSox pennant winner in the first year he ever managed a big league club? Adding that he would pilot five other big league teams makes this only a looping single.

4 A member of two Crimson Hose flag winners, he later managed the Sox for just one year and set the record for the most wins (90) by a skipper in his lone season as a big league helmsman. Triple, plus a RBI for the year.

5 Who piloted the Red Sox to a pennant but made the Hall of Fame in another non-playing capacity? RBI double, plus an extra RBI for his other job.

6 A Walpole, Mass., lad, this infielder wandered with six big league clubs in just four seasons as a part-timer. After he'd managed the Triple A Pawtucket PawSox for a team-record nine years, the BoSox finally gave him a midseason shot and promptly won their first 12 games under his stewardship before marching into the playoffs. RBI single, plus a second ribby for his magical year.

7 Who replaced Jimmy Collins at the Boston helm at the tail end of the 1906 season and thereupon became the club's second manager? Two-run double.

8 Four men took turns piloting the BoSox in 1907. Name the only one of the four who was no longer still an active player at the time and score a three-run homer.

9 Who managed the most recent Red Sox club to lose 100 games? Despite reaching the century mark, and placing 40 games out of first while allowing the most runs in the majors, the red hose didn't finish last. Double, plus a RBI for the year and an extra base for the club that ended up three games behind them.

10 What was the lone season in which the BoSox were piloted by not one but two men who had been catchers primarily in their active major league days? Four-bagger, plus a RBI for each manager named.

11 Whom did Jake Stahl replace at the Boston helm prior to the season in which Stahl guided the Sox to their second World Championship? Triple, plus a RBI for the year in question.

12 Who is the only man to have a .400 season in the majors and manage a Red Sox team? RBI double.

13 Name the lone man to steer the Sox for a full season to both a pennant and a last-place finish. Triple.

14 Many players have won bat crowns with the Sox, but only one such winner also managed them. Run it out for a double, plus a RBI for his year at the Hub helm.

15 What Hall of Famer managed a last-place Sox team that had a better record than the seventh-place Yankees team he had mentored exactly a decade earlier? Double, but up to a homer if you know both seasons involved.

AB: 15
Hits: 15
Total Bases: 39
RBI: 17

INNING 8
RED-HOT ROOKIES

1 By a margin of one home run in his official frosh season, he missed claiming the record for the fewest career dingers by a performer who hit 20 or more homers as a rookie. His 19 taters were accompanied by 96 RBI, but he ripped just one more four-bagger before disappearing in 1948. Solo seat-reacher for this World War II flying ace whose stay in Fenway lasted scarcely a year.

2 What BoSox rookie first sacker hit .310 in over 500 PA but bagged only one home run? Take a good look at this before you decide it has to be someone from the Deadball Era. Two bases for him, RBI for his rookie year.

3 Despite posting the lowest OPS ever (.586) for a Sox rookie with at least 400 PA, his sterling glove kept him in the 1914 lineup, as he tied for the AL frosh lead in games and led in at bats. A true mighty mite, he made his 148-pound frame last for over 1,600 big league games. RBI double.

4 Though arguably the AL's top frosh in his rookie season, this Red Sox gardener lost out in his bid to be declared the first official Rookie of the Year in AL history. However, he will always be the initial participant in a NCAA basketball tournament to appear in a ML game. A member of the 1943 NYU cagers, and the Violets leading scorer in the NCAA tourney, he took his last cuts with the 1956 Tribe. Two-base hit, plus a RBI for his rookie year.

5 Beckoned by the 1935 Sox after posting over 100 RBI three straight years with the San Francisco Missions of the PCL, a certain gateway guardian led AL rooks in walks and slapped 27 doubles. Displaced by Jimmie Foxx the next season, later this Frisco kid earned renown when he replaced a future Cooperstown inductee. RBI double.

6 Among rookies with at least 400 at bats in a season, he holds the post-1900 ML record for the highest BA at his position. His .331 yearling mark is 24 points above his 10-year career average. That season he stroked 165 singles, an AL frosh standard at that time. Double.

7 As a Boston AL rook in 1930 he hit a measly .185 in 54 games. He left the Sox after the 1933 season with a .213 BA, the lowest figure in team history of any infielder or outfielder that collected a minimum of 1,000 PA with the Sox. He rates a solo homer.

8 Since 1920, only one BoSox yearling pastureman has stroked .300 (minimum 400 at bats) while hitting fewer than 10 homers. During his career, exclusively in Sox garb, he pounded just 87 homers in 5,640 at bats. Double, plus a RBI for his frosh year.

9 Both the Sox and the Yankees had strapping six-foot lefty swingers take over their first-base posts on a full-time basis in 1925. By the close of the 1930 season, the Yanks could boast that they had gotten slightly the better of it as Lou Gehrig sported a .342 career BA to that point while the Sox gateway guardian stood at .259. How did this weak-stick lefty keep his job in red hosiery all that time? Good question, but we'll settle for his name here. Solo homer.

10 What rookie in the Red Sox 1952–1953 youth movement sent a grumbling Dom DiMaggio to the bench in the latter season when he played 136 games in center field and hit .283? Two-run homer.

11 When Ted Williams struck 31 home runs in 1939, whose club rookie dinger record did he break? Two-run homer.

12 What other Sox rookie in 1939 also broke the old frosh club record for home runs? Two-run double.

13 Babe Ruth, with four in 1915, holds the Sox record for the most dingers by a freshman pitcher. Who is the only other Sox rookie hurler to poke as many as three circuit clouts? He hit just .169 on the year but fashioned a nifty 13–8 figure before crashing to 2–9 as a soph in 1960. Two-run triple.

14 In 1955, Ted Williams led the Sox with 28 homers and Jackie Jensen was third on the club with 26. Sandwiched between them was a rookie first sacker who counted 27 taters among his 114 hits. Both figures represented about half of his career totals of 50 homers and 242 hits. Last seen with the 1959 Senators, he rates a two-run triple.

15 The Cleveland Browns wanted to groom him to succeed Otto Graham, but instead he chose baseball and became the only Red Sox yearling to reach double figures in dingers as a frosh and never hit another home run in the majors. Clues are slim, but the prize is high. Three-run homer.

AB: 15
Hits: 15
Total Bases: 44
RBI: 21

INNING 9
FALL CLASSICS

1 Manny Ramirez copped World Series MVP honors in 2004, but this Soxer, who batted .283 during the regular season, quietly outhit every other regular on both sides, stroking a cool .429. Double.

2 Name the Sox super sub who appeared in five World Series games between 1912 and 1916, four as a pinch hitter and the fifth as a pinch runner. In Game 8 of the 1912 Series, he had his big moment when he slashed a game-tying pinch double off the Giants' Christy Mathewson. Solo homer.

3 The Sox employed a pre-expansion postseason club-record 11 hurlers in the 1946 World Series. Which of these BoSox slab men from the mid-1940s was not among the 11? Bill Zuber, Mickey Harris, Mace Brown, Denny Galehouse, Clem Dreisewerd, Jim Bagby Jr. Double.

4 Dick Williams snuck him into three Series games in 1967, but this outfielder earlier saw October action with the Bombers in each of his first two major league campaigns. After a pathetic 2-for-30 showing with the BoSoxers in 1968, his 12-year big-top journey abruptly ended. Easy to get burned here, so we'll offer a two-run double.

5 The Red Sox received just one hit in 23 at bats from their two backstoppers in the 1946 World Series. Name the two receivers who hit a combined .043 and scored just one run and win yourself a two-run homer. Single if you know just one.

6 Who batted .176 for the Sox in the 1916 Series but led the team with six RBI and also clubbed the only two Boston homers? RBI double.

7 Babe Ruth set a still-existing World Series record for the longest single-game pitching stint when he went all 14 innings in a 4–3 win over Brooklyn in Game 2 of the 1916 classic. His catcher that day also caught an entire Series game the following afternoon. Who was that backstopper? Two-run homer.

8 Carl Yastrzemski rapped 10 hits in the 1967 World Series. Who was the only previous Red Sox performer to achieve a double-figure hit total in a Fall Classic? Triple.

9 The Red Sox used only three pitchers in the 1915 World Series, as they received complete-game outings in all five contests. Who was the only one of the trio to notch a complete-game loss, dropping the Series opener 3–1 to the Phils' Pete Alexander? RBI double.

10 Name the four Sox infielders in the 1912 Fall Classic, all of whom played every inning of every game. Homer for all four, single if you know only three.

11 In 1946 Mickey Harris became the second Sox hurler to lose two games in a Fall Classic. Who was the first Boston twirler to be painted with two defeats in a World Series? RBI triple.

12 Two catchers played in as many as three World Series with the Red Sox in the 1910s, yet neither appeared in the 1918 classic. One is a routine single; the other rates an extra two bases and a RBI even after we reveal his last name at birth was Bergland and he hit nary a home run in his 321 games in Sox threads.

13 This native of Puerto Rico became the first pitcher to blast a homer in his initial World Series at bat by victimizing the venerable Bob Gibson in the third inning of the 1967 opener. Dig for a generous two-bagger.

14 When Babe Ruth garnered his last World Series win in Game 4 of the 1918 classic, he finished the fray in left field, replacing George Whiteman. Who relieved Ruth in that game and not only garnered a save but finished the contest batting in Whiteman's cleanup spot in the order? RBI triple.

AB: 14
Hits: 14
Total Bases: 40
RBI: 13

GAME 5

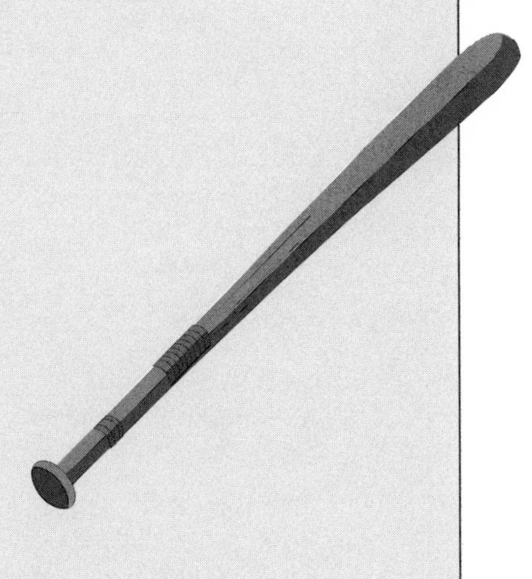

INNING 1
ALL IN THE FAMILY

1 The only sibling pitching tandem in Sox history to date had previously teamed up on a NL club. Both were 20-game winners during their careers, but only one reached the "charmed circle" in Crimson Hose. Single.

2 He was an AL All-Star selection in 1940, his first full season with the Sox, thanks to his .320 BA, while splitting his duties between first base and right field. He finished his career with the 1947 Phils by going 0-for-4, but that hardly compared to his brother's dreadful finish 11 years earlier with the Pirates. In 1936 the older sib was an unparalleled 0-for-35 in his fifth and final year as a Corsairs receiver, giving him the current record for the most AB in a season by a position player who failed to get a hit. Homer for the family name, and two extra RBI if you know both brothers' first names.

3 These Sox slammers blasted a sibling teammate record of 54 homers one season. That year they also became the first brothers to connect in the same AL game as teammates, and they did it twice no less. RBI single for them and an extra base for their record-setting season.

4 Which of the five Delahanty brothers was the only one ever to participate in an official AL game in Fenway Park? RBI single.

5 Both halves of the first brother battery in Red Sox history were over 30 when they initially played the point positions together with the Sox in 1929. The pitching bro began his career with the 1924 Yankees and was 20–17 after his first two seasons in the bigs. But in his remaining nine seasons he sagged to 77–147, including 27–52 in his three campaigns with the Sox. Historians will waltz to a two-run double here for the family name.

6 On July 19, 1933, these two brothers became the first pair of siblings in AL history to go deep in the same game. What's more, the BoSox half of the pair picked one of his bro's slants to pickle. Clues are enough to single here.

7 Dad is in the Hall of Fame. In 1956 papa's son teamed with BoSox receiver Sammy White to form the only ML battery to date that included a pair of teammates who had both played in a NCAA basketball tournament. Son's school was Princeton; dad had attended Michigan before signing his first professional contract. Double for the family, plus an extra base if you know both first names.

8 The son saw World Series action as a rookie in 1954. The father saw little but last place in his two seasons as a utility infielder with the Red Sox in 1929–1930. Dad finished his ML career with a .235 season. Son began his career by holding AL hitters to a minuscule .189 BA and topped that two years later when enemy batters rapped just .170 against him, leading to a 1.52 ERA in 32 relief appearances. The family name will garner you a three-bagger; knowing both first names is worth two RBI.

9 Sometimes it skips a generation, as this grandpa can attest after roaming the BoSox pasture for five years during the 1920s before managing the club in the early 1930s. His grandson debuted with the 1972 Sox but quickly slipped to the Astros and Mets, finishing with a .220 BA in 213 career games. They hailed from Massachusetts and carried different surnames, so we'll award a homer for both, just a double for one.

10 He was a BoSox backstopper for five seasons, ending in 1930. His younger brother served as a Sox hillman for three seasons at the end of the decade of the 1930s and was a fine 31–11 while wearing Crimson Hose. In 1944 the younger sib led all AL slab men in appearances at age 44 with 63. Two-run homer.

11 Papa caught for the Sox and batted a woeful .161 over parts of four seasons in Boston, while sonny boy eked out a .169 BA in five partial campaigns behind Fenway's dish. Some may think that daddy's front-office job with the Sox helped the kid last longer in the show than his weak bat merited. RBI single.

12 A Sox regular for two seasons at short, he later managed the Dodgers, but his pitching brother who debuted with the Marlins in 1993 would make the family name far more famous. RBI single.

13 Replacing an injured Yankees regular, he led both participants in the 1978 World Series with a .438 BA while his twin brother Blake stalled in Triple A. An elder and more famous sib of theirs played every game for the BoSox in the 1975 Fall Classic before these boys started a successful baseball camp in Winter Haven, Florida. Single for the family name.

14 This Sox pennant-winning double-play combo each had a sibling who also played the same position as his brother in the majors. One of the Sox sibs saw action with the Phils and missed platooning at second in Boston with his bro by a year. The other sib played 92 career games, mostly as a backup at short with the Cubs. Score a double for nailing both BoSox middle infielders, plus an extra base each for their brothers.

AB: 14
Hits: 14
Total Bases: 32
RBI: 14

INNING 2
RBI RULERS

1 Who is the only rapper in Red Sox history to register two 100 RBI seasons despite never tagging as many as 10 homers in any of his campaigns with the Red Sox? Solo homer.

2 Since World War II only one Soxer has plated 100 runs in consecutive seasons while hitting fewer than 20 homers in both campaigns. During the first of those years, this mustachioed contact swinger stroked 16 homers and a team-leading 110 RBI, followed by a career-best 18 homers with 102 ribbies. Single, plus a RBI for his two-year run.

3 What Hub star posted six 100 RBI seasons but never led the Sox in ribbies? Interestingly, this career Bostonian totaled his personal high (120) a year before leaving the big top. Double, plus a RBI for his highpoint year.

4 Jimmie Foxx and Buck Freeman were the first two performers to nail as many as two 100 RBI seasons for the Sox. Who was the third such batsman to do it? Solo homer because this is a lot harder than most of you may think.

5 To date, who is the only player to lead the Sox in ribbies during each of his first three seasons in the majors? Double, plus a RBI for knowing his three-year run.

6 Five years after serving as a key member of a club that defeated the Red Sox in Series play, he topped the Sox in RBI with 105 and in so doing became the oldest Soxer (38) to notch a 100-ribby season. RBI single.

7 Who is the only third sacker to date to top the Red Sox in RBI for two straight seasons? Although he plated 87 mates the first year and 95 the second, he drove home over 100 one year earlier in his career without pacing the club. Double, plus a RBI for his two-year run.

8 Prior to Rich Gedman, who was the only lefty-hitting catcher to total as many as 150 career RBI in Red Sox garb? Do yourself proud and strut to a three-run homer if you know this backstopper who romped with Foxx and the Thumper and finished with the 1945 Dodgers.

9 After leading the AL with 123 RBI at age 31, this Soxer never again qualified for the batting title and was through five years later. Cumulatively, he poled 251 seat-reachers, 113 of them coming in crimson flannels. RBI single, plus an extra base for the year he topped the junior loop in ribbies.

10 One of the performers who collected fewer than 1,000 at bats in Red Sox livery, his 172 RBI lead all, even though he's currently only tied for 12th on the same club list in total bases. The era in which he played for the Sox had much to do with his RBI total. Home run.

11 Naming the first Sox freshman to pace the club outright in RBI since Ted Williams in 1939 will earn you a trip to second, plus a RBI for the year.

12 What Sox slugger had a season in which he bagged 103 RBI and slammed 19 homers but scored only 45 runs, the fewest ever by a 100 RBI man? RBI double, plus an extra base for the year in question.

13 Over a 12-season career, all of it spent in crimson gear, this sweet swinger's RBI total reached the century mark just once, but his 119 ribbies that year topped the team. Double.

14 When Ted Williams notched 34 RBI in 1953 in only 91 at bats, whose club record did he break for most RBI with fewer than 100 AB? The record formerly belonged to a Hall of Famer and former teammate of Ted's. Two bases.

AB: 14
Hits: 14
Total Bases: 35
RBI: 14

INNING 3
CY YOUNG SIZZLERS

1 A pitcher on a last-place team has next to no chance of winning a Cy Young Award. What hurler on the 1923 cellar edition of the Red Sox would unquestionably have received at least a smattering of votes for the honor had it been in existence when he tied for fourth in the loop in wins and was second in both complete games and innings? RBI two-bagger.

2 Although the Sox won the AL pennant, only one Boston moundsman earned a Cy Young vote in 1975. Make your most intelligent choice for a double.

3 Apart from Babe Ruth in 1916, who is the only Sox southpaw prior to expansion that would have been an almost certain Cy Young winner based on his loop lead in wins and complete games? Triple, plus a RBI for his big year.

4 In 1939 the Sox finished second to the Yanks despite not having a single hurler that worked as many as 200 innings. What 39-year-old tosser led the BoSox in frames with 191 and also paced the AL in winning percentage, thanks to his glittering 15–4 mark and loop-best 2.54 ERA? An earlier retrospective Cy Young winner, he would have received strong support again in 1939 despite his slim wins and innings totals. Double.

5 A 21–6 slate for a world champ is a pretty nifty credential for a Cy Young candidate, but a certain BoSox ace with that glistening record finished second in that year's balloting, failing to capture a single first-place vote. RBI single.

6 In 1917 Babe Ruth led the Red Sox with 24 wins, but he probably would not have been the club's leading vote getter had there been a Cy Young Award that year. What 22-game winner would have, thanks to his club-leading .710 winning percentage and 1.74 ERA? Later a teammate of Ruth's on the Yankees, he's worth a RBI double.

7 The first Crimson Hose reliever to notch a Cy Young vote went 13–9 in 69 appearances that season with a 2.96 ERA. No soup in your lunch bucket if you fail to single, but we'll add an extra base to the broth for also nailing the year.

8 The 1915 Red Sox were the first flag winner in AL history without a 20-game winner. Who in all probability would have been the club's top vote getter for AL pitching honors, owing to his 1.64 ERA and 19 wins? Triple.

9 The first Sox lefty to earn Cy Young votes placed fifth that year for a glittering 18–6 season. It proved to be his last of nine seasons in Fenway, as he exited after inking a free-agent deal in the senior circuit. Single, plus a RBI for the year he earned 12 votes in BoSox garb.

10 Beginning in 1967, a Cy Young winner was chosen each year in both leagues. Since that season, who has notched the most career victories to date in Sox garb without ever earning a single Cy Young vote? RBI double.

11 Since the Cy Young Award's inception in 1956, who was the first BoSox 20-game winner that failed to earn a single vote? The majors only chose one winner back then, and writers were limited to marking just one choice each, accounting in part for his complete omission from the balloting. RBI single.

12 Shouldn't take you long to name the first BoSoxer to capture all the writers' first-place votes for that year's Cy Young voting. Scratch single, plus a RBI for the year of his unanimous selection.

13 After spending three seasons with another AL club, this starter arrived in Boston and earned Cy Young votes in each of his first two Beantown campaigns but never earned another vote in Red Sox threads. However, he would later win the Cy Young with another AL outfit. Single.

14 Who was the first BoSoxer to garner a Cy Young vote in two separate decades? Although he started 15 or more games three times in Beantown, this Maine man came out of the Sox pen 500+ times more often than he appeared in their rotation. Single.

AB: 14
Hits: 14
Total Bases: 24
RBI: 8

INNING 4
ODD COMBO ACHIEVEMENTS

Babe Ruth held the ML records for both the most career home runs and the most career batters strikeouts when he retired. In this section, you'll meet former Red Sox who also hold odd and often contradictory club and ML records.

1 On three occasions this Sox swatter topped the AL in homers, but fewer Crimson Hose rooters know that he also stroked the most triples in a season by a BoSoxer since WWII. Scurry to first.

2 Five years after this BoSox ace shared the AL lead in victories, he set the team season mark for losses in fewer than 160 innings. The possessor of a true Jekyll and Hyde career, he went a nifty 75–53 in his first six seasons and an atrocious 22–47 thereafter. RBI double.

3 We find the same first and last name in the BoSox club record book for both the lowest season batting average by a position player with a minimum of 100 plate appearances (.075) and the most losses in a season by a pitcher in fewer than 90 innings (11).

Yet the record holder in each case is *not* the same player. The hitter was an easily forgotten catcher who achieved his .075 mark in 1931 but nonetheless saw semiregular duty the following year before exiting the majors. The slabster set the loss mark as a rookie lefty in 1964 and fashioned a shutout in his lone career complete game. Three-run homer.

4 The Red Sox all-time season leader in RBI (90) in a year in which he failed to hit a single home run also ranked first in career RBI when he completed his tour in Boston, where he spent the first eight seasons of an 11-year ML sojourn. Last seen with the 1921 Senators, the owner of this odd record combo is worth a double.

5 Among pitchers who started at least 20 games in a season for the Sox since the end of the Deadball Era, his .211 winning percentage is the absolute worst, and he coupled it with an ERA just over 5.00. A bum, right? Not quite, since he also holds the all-time club record for the highest single-season winning percentage (.882) among those with at least 15 wins. Single.

6 Which of the following diverse Red Sox club records is the only one Tris Speaker did not hold when he left Boston in 1916? Doubles, stolen bases, walks, errors by an outfielder, games played, assists by an outfielder, hit by pitch. RBI single.

7 True or false: When Babe Ruth left Boston, he held the Sox club records for both the most home runs and the most pitching wins by a left-hander. If true, who was the runner-up to him in each department? If false, who was the leader in the department or departments he didn't capture. Triple.

8 When Ted Williams returned from World War II in 1946, he held a wide assortment of Sox career records among players with a minimum of 1,000 at bats in Hub garb. Which among the following is the only one he did not hold? Batting average, slugging average, home run percentage, on base percentage, runs created per game. RBI single.

9 Who among retired players currently holds both the Sox season record for the most stolen bases by a catcher and the Sox career record for the highest on base percentage among players with a minimum of 1,000 plate appearances that hit below .300 with the Sox? Two-run double.

10 The same performer owns the Sox career records for both the fewest walks (81) and the fewest strikeouts (49) among all hitters with a minimum of 2,000 at bats in Crimson Hose. Cram a RBI triple into your account by naming this frequent World Series participant.

11 The lone hurler to log 1,000 innings apiece with both Boston in the AL and the NL is also the lone performer to team with the Babe on the Bronx Bombers *and* play for the Braves the year Ruth retired. Born in North Truro, Mass., the owner of this odd combo is good for three bases.

12 Usually players who steal bases have an edge when it comes to rapping triples, owing to their speed. However, this Soxer, despite leading the AL in steals one year and pacing the Crimson Hose cumulatively in thefts in a certain decade, became the first ALer with a minimum of 600 PA to go without hitting a three-bagger in two consecutive seasons. Double for the holder of this odd record combo.

13 Although he once held the BoSox career record for hits with a mark that stood for 25 years after his retirement, this lefty swinger also posted the pre-expansion club standard for the lowest season BA (minimum 500 plate appearances) by an outfielder. Prior to expansion, he sported the Sox' second worst season BA among pasturemen too, but who's counting? We hope you are, because he's good for two bases.

14 Two performers since 1900 participated in 300 or more games with both the Boston Red Sox and the Boston Braves. Combined, they played 30 seasons in the majors, and each collected at least 4,000 at bats. Between them, they accumulated over 3,000 hits but rapped only 31 homers. Each weighed less than 165 pounds, and they played for other teams besides Boston in both major leagues. Yet they were never teammates and never played against each other in a ML game. Zapping both men will bring a RBI triple. Sac fly RBI if you know just one of them.

AB: 14
Hits: 14
Total Bases: 30
RBI: 9

INNING 5
BRAZEN BASE THIEVES

1 The first Boston performer to win an AL theft crown perpetrated the feat in his only full season in Sox threads. Later he won an AL bat title, and you can win a standup double, plus a RBI for his victory theft year.

2 Swiping at least 20 bags twice in Sox finery during a decade when no other BoSoxer did it even once, this outfielder managed to lead the AL in one of those years. RBI single, plus an extra base for the year he topped the junior loop.

3 The first Red Soxer to cop two AL theft crowns and the initial third baseman in AL history to win back-to-back steal titles are one and the same and rate a RBI single.

4 What Soxer set the ML mark for lowest season total ever to lead a major league in steals? This one's been tossed around the horn a bit, but we'll still offer a double for him, plus a RBI for the year, and an extra base for his total.

5 Nail the first BoSoxer to swipe as many as 40 bases in a season and snare a three-bagger, plus a RBI for his big year.

6 Who set a Sox documented club record in 1914 when he was nabbed 31 times trying to steal? Double.

7 The Sox season club mark for steals was set by a man who topped the AL that year and snagged over 100 sacks during the three campaigns he roamed Fenway's pasture. Single, plus a RBI for the year he set the Sox swipe standard.

8 Prior to the above man, who had owned the Sox season theft record for some 60 years with a total of 52? Single for him, plus a RBI for his year.

9 What Sox great holds the club career steals record? Double for him, plus an extra base if you can come within five of his record total.

10 He collected 1,092 career at bats in Sox livery and was the only Soxer prior to expansion to possess as many as 1,000 at bats and 0 stolen bases. Three-bagger.

11 Historically, Red Sox teams have not relied on speed, and a certain performer's feat crystallizes this fact. He is the only Soxer since the days of the Grey Eagle to have stolen as many as 30 bases in successive seasons. Wildly popular during his four-year Fenway stay, this flychaser drew many "Disciples." Cinch single.

12 Had a strike not curtailed the 1994 season, this journeyman outfielder may have topped the Sox record for steals, as he totaled 42 with 37 games left on the schedule. However, his weak stick produced a woeful .677 OPS that year in over 400 plate appearances and a pink slip from Boston brass after just one season. Double.

13 From 1938 to 1971 only one BoSoxer swiped as many as 25 bases in a season. But like many other hitters that year, he did little else, poking just .225 and slugging a pitiful .326, the lowest seasonal SA ever by a Sox qualifier at his position (502 plate appearances) since the Crash of 1929. Double, plus a RBI for the year.

14 Who posted the highest season stolen base total in a Sox uniform among these longtime Crimson stalwarts? Carl Yastrzemski, Reggie Smith, Nomar Garciaparra, John Valentin, Gary Geiger, Jackie Jensen. Double.

AB: 14
Hits: 14
Total Bases: 27
RBI: 8

INNING 6
HOME RUN KINGS

1 Babe Ruth left Boston with 49 career home runs. His 49th and final blast in Sox garb broke Buck Freeman's club record for the most career round-trippers. What longtime teammate of Freeman's stood second on the team's career dinger list when he left the Hub after the 1907 season? Take four bases and our praise for having earned every one of them.

2 His 17 homers for a BoSox flag winner were the most by a Soxer at his position in 34 years. In his less than two full seasons in Fenway threads, he pounded 24 seat-reachers before moving on. Double for him, a RBI for the season, plus an extra ribby for his position.

3 The last Soxer to date that collected 500 at bats in a season without reaching the seats also became the most recent Sox stick to accrue 600 homerless at bats when he did it the previous year. Actually, this Fall River, Mass., product failed to go deep in his last 2,292 career at bats. Nonetheless, he remains a Beantown fan favorite. Double.

4 Prior to Jimmie Foxx's arrival in the Hub, who held the BoSox season record for the most circuit clouts by a right-handed hitter? Would you believe this is tough enough to rate a two-run homer, plus an extra RBI for his record season?

5 Beginning as a starting pitcher in the Cards' chain, he went 20–7 in 1955 with Hamilton in the PONY League before leading the Sox with 18 clouts six years later as their regular center fielder in the AL's first expansion season. Constant health problems and injuries, including a collapsed lung, a fractured skull, and recurring ulcers, kept him from fulfilling his early promise. RBI double.

6 The first clubber to whack at least 30 homers in a season in both leagues achieved that feat by mashing a team-leading 42 missiles in his first year with Boston after pounding 35 dingers two years earlier for a senior-loop club. Most fans would find it strange if we offered more than a RBI single here.

7 Joe Cronin was the first performer who was primarily a shortstop to slug 100 home runs in Sox garb. Who was the second to do so? Like Cronin, he too finished with 105 in crimson hosiery and played other infield positions at times. RBI single.

8 Name the first switch-hitter to clock 100 homers in a Red Sox uniform. Unhappy about his treatment in Boston, he pushed the Sox to deal him when he was only 28 and still had plenty of pop left in his lumber. Single.

9 Upon their mutual retirement in 1976, this pair stood 1–2 all-time in lowest career BA among ML sluggers with 200+ homers. One stroked an uninspiring .244, popped 245 seat-reachers, and played parts of his last three seasons with the Sox. The other thrilled Fenway faithful for years, batting .251 with 210 career clouts. Three bases for both these bammers, zilch for just one.

10 In 11 campaigns this Puerto Rico native poked just 89 homers in 969 games. However, he went wild in his first full year in Fenway, setting a record, later tied, for fewest RBI (64) by a player who cranked at least 30 homers in a season. Double, plus an extra base for the year he tattooed the Green Monster.

11 The first catcher to slug as many as 15 home runs in his career with the Sox totaled 16 as a Hub backstopper and resides in Cooperstown. RBI single.

12 What outfielder paced the Sox with 21 dingers one season and then crushed 40 six years later with a NL outfit but failed to lead his new team? Of course, the latter club's rarefied air helped this Mississippi masher; nevertheless, he belted over 30 taters with two other teams as well. Single, plus a RBI for the year he topped the BoSox in seat-reachers.

13 Nowadays this dubious feat is commonplace, but who was the only BoSox slugger prior to AL expansion to have a season in which he smacked as many as 25 jacks despite hitting under .250? Three bases, plus a RBI for the year he did it.

AB: 13
Hits: 13
Total Bases: 28
RBI: 11

INNING 7
RED-HOT ROOKIES

1 Shoulder fatigue prevented this former Mississippi State flamethrower from breaking the all-time frosh save record, shelving him after September 1. Keep yourself off the DL and nail him for a single, plus a RBI for the year.

2 The first BoSox receiver to homer in double figures as a rookie went deep just 66 times in an 11-year career that ended with the 1962 Phils. Who is he? Double.

3 When Tris Speaker took over the Sox centerfield post in 1909, he replaced a two-year Boston vet who had debuted with the club in 1907 by posting a .283 slugging average, the lowest ever by a Sox regular outfielder. Who was this plywood lumber rookie? Three-run homer.

4 Despite leading all ML rookies in runs, walks, and OBP while playing on a Sox pennant winner, this middle infielder inexplicably failed to earn a single vote in that year's AL rookie balloting. RBI single.

5 In 1901 what infielder played every game for the AL Hub entry and hit .306, which proved to be the highest BA by a Boston AL rookie (minimum 500 plate appearances) in the Deadball Era? RBI double.

6 A cup of coffee with the Braves was all this 26-year-old shortstop had tasted of the show when he went to spring training with the BoSox in 1955. He not only won the Hub job but rapped a solid .283. The following year the Sox moved him to third base but then returned him to short in 1957 when Frank Malzone arrived. Never again a regular after 1957, he finished with the 1963 Phils, a year before his brother made his ML debut with Cincinnati. Who is he? Solo homer.

7 Who holds the Sox club mark for homers in a season by a player who collected fewer than 200 at bats? Looming 6'5" and weighing over 215 pounds, he looked even bigger at the plate, slamming 14 round-trippers as a freshman in just 158 at bats. That year, he also blasted 30 for Pawtucket in the International League, just one behind the IL loop leader. Although never fulfilling his early promise, this Texan's popularity grew after he became a Sox post-game cable analyst. Single, plus a RBI for the year of his freshman rampage.

8 Averaging 10 Ks per nine innings by fanning 155 in just 139⅓ frames, a certain Soxer actually set the club frosh mark (since broken) for strikeouts three years *after* he had toiled for them in World Series action. Well traveled, this southpaw's ML ride ended in 1981 with over 150 games apiece as both a starter and a reliever. RBI single.

9 The first Sox freshman to pop 20 homers and swipe 20 bases is also the initial team member to snag 20 sacks in each of his first three ML seasons. Twelve years after exiting Boston, this former NL All-Star returned to take his final cuts in Crimson Hose. RBI single, plus an extra base for his frosh season.

10 Called up after winning the International League MVP and *The Sporting News* Minor League Player of the Year honors, this Soxer topped all ML yearling batting-title qualifiers in OPS (.778). Sadly, he never played another game for the Sox after age 25, and three years later he was gone from the bigs. Double, plus a RBI for his rookie year.

11 He led all rooks in games, homers, and ribbies but failed to cop the AL frosh award. A free swinger, he also set the yearling mark (later broken) for strikeouts with 152. RBI single, plus an extra base for the year.

12 In 1929 a certain Red Sox frosh led the club in at bats, triples, hits, total bases, and RBI. His 17 three-baggers marked the last time to date that a Sox hitter stroked more than 15. A promise of great things to come? Nope. After one more season in the Sox garden, he served out most of the rest of his days in the minors. Two-run homer.

13 Born in the Bronx and raised near Yankee Stadium, this 21-year-old Sox slinger went 12–2, earning the *Sporting News* AL Rookie Pitcher of the Year Award. After 20 starts as a sophomore, he never again worked regularly, drifting briefly to the Cards and Astros before vanishing at age 26. RBI double, plus an extra base for his freshman year.

14 The Sox pitching during most of the 1920s was nothing short of frightful. One arm that showed promise belonged to a righty who came from Washington late in the 1924 season. In 1925, his official frosh campaign, he led the Sox with 12 wins and set a club record that will almost surely never be broken when he averaged just 1.06 strikeouts for every nine innings he worked. Two years later, in his coda ML season, he set an all-time record for the fewest strikeouts by a pitcher in a minimum of 70 innings when he K'd a mere one batter in 74⅔ frames for the Sox. His name suggested that he might be a hard thrower, but his arm said otherwise. Two-run homer.

15 Before Daisuke Matsuzaka, it had been a while since the BoSox sported a freshman flinger who notched at least 10 wins, and we'll wager a double, plus a RBI for the year, that you'll get nipped in the bud trying to nail this righty who went 11–6 with a 3.89 ERA.

AB: 15
Hits: 15
Total Bases: 35
RBI: 18

INNING 8
THE NAME'S THE SAME

There has been only one performer in Red Sox history named Ruth and only one Speaker, Yastrzemski, and Parnell. But there have been multiple Smiths, Williamses, and Wilsons. The questions in this category depict two or more Red Sox players with the same last name. Test yourself on your ability to determine the last and first names of the players involved in each case.

1 The BoSox' primary center fielder in 1998, their regular left fielder in 1912, and their leading loser in 1901. RBI double.

2 The Sox center fielder in 1994, the Boston outfielder who hit .306 in 2003, and the righty who notched 12 victories with three shutouts for the 1955 Fenway crew. Double, but you need all three first names to score here.

3 The southpaw reliever who posted a 10–4 record with the 1948 Red Sox, the club's RBI leader in 1934, and the club's RBI leader in 1944. Need all three for a triple, single for only two.

4 The backstopper who caught more than half of the Red Sox games in both 1915 and 1916, the Sox gardener who saw action in the 1967 World Series, and the White Sox mound mainstay in the late 1920s and early 1930s who finished his career with the 1937 Red Sox. Home run for all three, single for only two.

5 A hurler who dropped 21 games one year for an AL last-place finisher that represented Beantown and a first baseman who ripped .335 one year for a Boston AL cellar dweller shared *both* the same first and last names. What was that name? Two-bagger.

6 The Sox' regular receiver in 1946, their regular shortstop in 1912, and a 14-game BoSox winner in 1942. Two-run homer for all three, single for only two.

7 A backup outfielder with the 1918 BoSox who hit .352 four years later for the Cubs, a Sox infielder who played over 100 games in both 1930 and 1931, and the Sox outfielder in 1974 who bagged only 22 RBI in 114 games. Tough enough to rate a double for just the last name. Three-run homer if you also know all three first names.

8 An All-American quarterback who never quite was able to earn the Sox catching job in the late 1950s and early 1960s, a center fielder who earned a ticket to Cleveland late in the 1908 season after logging a meager .276 on base percentage in 101 games for the Sox, and the hurler who finished his eight-year stint with the Sox by earning just six wins in 22 decisions in 1960. Two-run homer for all three, single for only two.

9 The regular second sacker on a memorable Sox World Series loser, the BoSox' 1944 closer who finished in the AL's top five with eight saves, and the 1907 Hub outfielder who played over 100 games after previously rapping .300+ twice with the Tigers. Three-run shot for the trio, double for two, otherwise zip.

10 A Sox chucker who went 10–4 in 1919 after arriving in a major midseason swap with the Yanks, a 20-game loser for the awful 1930 BoSox outfit, and the closer who once saved 33 games for Butch Hobson's gang. Homer for all three, single for just two.

11 The Sox' regular first baseman in 1934 who hit .350+ for Cleveland one season earlier in the decade, a Red Sox chucker who won 14 games in 1908 and later bagged 33 more for two Connie Mack pennant winners, and a rookie Sox skipper who guided them to the postseason. Homer for all three, single for just two.

12 The 1916 Sox center fielder who later topped the AL in homers with another club, the future 11-year vet who replaced Carl Yastrzemski in left during Yaz's last ML game, and the Sox' regular second sacker in 2003 who scored 92 runs. Triple for the trio, single for only two.

13 A 1937 BoSox starter-reliever who finished second in the junior loop with 51 games, a Sox rookie who started over 20 games in 1945 and later tossed the first no-hitter by a member of the Milwaukee Braves, and the performer who led the 1965 Red Sox in wins. Triple for all three, single for just two.

14 The Vermont native who bagged 20 wins for the 1914 Sox, the Massachusetts-born outfielder who hit .286 for the 1921 BoSox, and the Soxer who hailed from New York State and earned a plaque in Cooperstown in 1945. Triple for all three, single for only two.

AB: 14
Hits: 14
Total Bases: 46
RBI: 14

INNING 9
MASTER MOUNDSMEN

1 Who is the only 20-game winner to date that served exclusively as a starter and tossed fewer than 200 innings? Not Bob Grim, he worked 17 games from the pen when he nailed 20 with the Yanks in 1954. What's more, Grim couldn't hold a candle to our guy, who started 30 games and posted a scintillating .833 winning percentage. Scratch single.

2 Between 1988 and 1996, Roger Clemens started Opening Day for the Sox every year except one. Who got that starting nod in place of the Rocket? The pride of Golden Valley, Minnesota, he bagged only three wins that year, including the season lid-lifter. But he later led the Sox in victories once and won 69 games during a four-year stretch for another AL club. Single for him; ribby for the year he started a Sox opener.

3 Since Lefty Grove in 1936, only one other Sox southpaw has been a league leader in shutouts. Sharing the AL crown with five whitewashes, he also tied for the club lead in wins that campaign. RBI double, plus an extra base for the season he led.

4 This one's tough. The lone Sox 20-game winner prior to expansion without a shutout to his credit cracked the "charmed circle" in his rookie year and never made it again. Clues are right for the obliging to score a triple.

5 What was Babe Ruth's biggest win season for the Sox, and how many victories did he have? One base for the year, plus a RBI for the win total.

6 Who was the first Red Sox hurler since the Deadball Era (minimum one inning pitched per team game played) to hold the opposition to a BA under .200? Single, plus a RBI for the year.

7 What Cooperstown inductee's only game as a BoSoxer was his last, a starting assignment against the team with whom he had previously starred? Born in North Adams, Mass., he died in that state on his farm in Conway. Double, plus a RBI for the year he sported crimson threads.

8 Between 1954 and 1969, this former NL 20-game winner was the only Sox lefty to win at least 10 games in a season when he went 16–7. However, he never earned another victory in crimson threads, as he was packaged with Ken Harrelson in that stormy deal to the Tribe. Double.

9 The Sox prize in the Ken Harrelson swap, he once led Boston with 16 victories and four shutouts after notching 29 wins over his previous two Beantown seasons. Although never again as effective, this Missouri moundsman added 12 more wins before bouncing around with four other clubs the next four seasons. RBI single for one of the rare post-WWII Sox hurlers who could also hit a bit.

10 Who won the most career games among Crimson Hose slab men that never toiled on a Sox flag winner? A notorious lover of home cooking, he went 71–30 at Fenway alone. RBI single.

11 The last Soxer to log 300 innings in a season tossed 25 complete games that year, winning a career-high 22. At one point, this workhorse featured six different pitches, and you need to slap one of them to gain a RBI single, plus an extra base for the year.

12 Numerologists will dig this colorful BoSox southpaw who won exactly 17 games for three straight seasons, the last one coming with a Fenway flag winner. Single.

13 To date, the oldest Red Sox twirler to notch a double-figure win season was 42 when he bagged 15 victories in his lone full season in Fenway. Single, plus a RBI for the year.

14 Cy Young started at least 35 games for the Crimson Hose in each of their first four campaigns. Many years passed until the next BoSox chucker turned the same trick four straight seasons, and he did it 10 years after Young died. Never the same after that huge early workload, this righty later bagged 11 wins over parts of two seasons in pinstripes. Two-run single.

AB: 14
Hits: 14
Total Bases: 21
RBI: 11

GAME 6

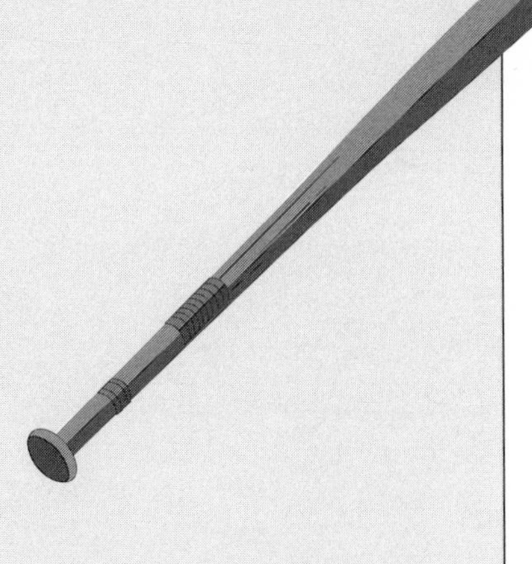

INNING 1
HOME RUN KINGS

1 Oh, sure, you know all about that Deadball Era slugger who debuted with the BoSox and then was sold elsewhere, only to become a loop leader in homers six times during a seven-year stretch, with his last four-bagger crown coming at age 38. But how sure of yourself are you, really? No curse here, but you'll utter several if our clues take you down the wrong path. Double.

2 The rapper who holds the career record for homers by a teenager also owns the AL mark for the youngest performer to reach 100 taters. Effortless single for Sox devotees.

3 Excluding Teddy Ballgame, whose streak was interrupted by military service, who holds the Sox record for most consecutive seasons with at least 20 homers? This one's tougher than it looks, so we'll ante a double, plus an extra base for knowing the years his streak ran.

4 Who is the only bammer to date that led the junior circuit in home runs with Boston and also had another season in which he topped the senior loop in taters? Triple.

5 Slap a RBI single for naming the first Soxer to poke 20 jacks in a season without playing so much as a single inning in the field that year.

6 Who were the only two performers prior to AL expansion in 1961 to tag at least 100 career home runs and 50 triples with the Red Sox? RBI single.

7 Who posted the lowest BA during a 40-homer season in Red Sox garb? That year, he also set a ML record (later broken) for the lowest SA (.507) for a 40-tater clubber. Single, plus a RBI for the year.

8 The first to clear the present location of the Green Monster twice in his career, he also became the first to clear it three times in 1916 when he hit the Sox' lone homer of the season at home in his initial year in Beantown. He left the majors in 1923 with the most career home runs in AL history to that point by a right-handed hitter. RBI double.

9 This slugger dug home cooking so much that he set the current season mark for taters at Fenway, powering a whopping 20 more in Boston than he did on the road. Bound for Cooperstown, he led the AL that year, but his career-best dinger campaign came with another outfit. Two-run single.

10 Who set the BoSox season record for the fewest walks (27) by a player that poled at least 30 homers? Later a manager, he became the first Crimson Hose helmsman in over 60 years to lead the club to three straight losing seasons. Single for him, plus a RBI for the year of his dubious offensive achievement.

11 The only Red Sox receiver to blast 20 round-trippers in a season in fewer than 400 at bats powered 21 in 349 AB, plus three more combined as a DH and pinch hitter. During his career, he had two separate stints each with the Sox and the Bombers, exiting after the 2000 campaign. RBI single, plus an extra base for the year.

12 A certain Sox backup catcher collected just four pinch hits in 1953, but he made them count by sending each safely over the fence to lead the majors in substitute blasts. Name him and earn a homer of your own.

13 In his two years at Fenway this hulking slugger powered 24 dingers and followed with 28 more despite collecting fewer than 400 at bats in both campaigns. Telling you that he formerly copped an AL MVP with another club lowers this controversial star's name to a single.

14 Excluding first sackers, DHs, and outfielders, who has the highest career home run percentage per 100 at bats among Soxers with a minimum of 1,000 plate appearances? RBI two-bagger.

AB: 14
Hits: 14
Total Bases: 25
RBI: 10

INNING 2
STELLAR STICKWIELDERS

1 Nomar Garciaparra left the Sox with a .323 career batting average. Which performer with a club record for the highest BA (.326) with at least 1,000 plate appearances at shortstop did he threaten before ending up three points shy of the mark? RBI single.

2 To date, who is the only receiver to accumulate 1,000 or more at bats with the Red Sox and finish with a .300 career BA for his time served in the Hub? RBI double.

3 Prior to AL expansion in 1961, just one third baseman with a minimum of 1,000 at bats in Sox garb posted a .300 career BA while at the hot corner. For a triple, who was it?

4 What Red Sox performer was denied a Triple Crown when he finished second in batting by a margin of less than one percentage point? Single for the hitter, plus two ribbies for the year.

5 The lone man prior to Tris Speaker with a minimum of 1,000 at bats as a member of the Boston AL club to depart with a .300 career BA in Beantown threads finished his Hub tour at .325. Name him for a two-run double.

6 The worst career batting average in Hub history among performers with a minimum of 2,000 plate appearances as a member of the Boston AL entry belongs to what early-day worthy? Three bases.

7 Ted Williams posted eight of the BoSox top 10 season walk totals to date. Who are the only other Sox stickmen to draw at least 120 walks in a campaign and thus make the top-10 list? Each is worth a single base.

8 Who was the first man to collect 1,000 career hits for the Boston AL entry? RBI triple.

9 Seven Soxers prior to AL expansion in 1961 compiled .300 BAs coupled with an OPS below .800 in a minimum of 1,000 plate appearances. Name all seven of these seldom walk, little power, high BA guys and nab a grand slam. Triple for six, single for five.

10 Common today but once very rare were performers with season OBPs over .400 despite posting sub-.300 batting averages. The Sox' first such batsman with a .400 OBP and a sub-.300 BA with a minimum of 400 plate appearances was a member of the 1936 club. His line included a .401 OBP and a .273 BA and earned him a trip to the minors in 1937 before returning for his ML finale with the 1938 Reds. Name him for a grand-slam homer.

11 Name the three stickmen who compiled .500+ slugging averages coupled with sub-.300 batting averages in two or more seasons as Red Sox regulars prior to AL expansion in 1961. Double for all three, zip for less than three.

12 Three first basemen prior to AL expansion in 1961 logged .300 career BAs with a minimum of 1,000 AB in Sox threads. Name all three and score a triple. Single for two, and naught for just one.

13 The only Soxer to slap 200 hits in the same season he coaxed 100 or more walks did it four consecutive years. You should rap a clean single here, but we'll add an extra sack for nailing his four-year run.

14 What future Hall of Famer topped the Pacific Coast League in hits while playing for San Diego the year before he joined the

Sox? We'll go a double that you'll open the wrong entry to the answer.

15 Deadball Era mavens will breeze to a standup triple here. The rest may struggle even to put this sharp-breaking curve in play. Prior to 1920, the close of the Deadball Era, only one BoSox infielder—first basemen included—enjoyed as many as four seasons in the Hub in which he had collected 200 or more total bases. Name him.

AB: 15
Hits: 15
Total Bases: 37
RBI: 15

INNING 3
MEMORABLE MONIKERS

1 Hawk. RBI single.

2 Rooster. Single.

3 Hoot. Triple.

4 Spaceman. Single.

5 Birdie. Double.

6 The Major. RBI single.

7 Rabbit. RBI double.

8 Roxy. Home run.

9 Dr. Strangeglove. Single.

10 The Little Professor. RBI single.

11 Nig. Triple.

12 The Rocket. An excuse me swing single.

13 Hick. Home run.

14 Big Papi. Baltimore chop single.

15 Sea Lion. RBI triple.

AB: 15
Hits: 15
Total Bases: 29
RBI: 7

INNING 4
BULLPEN BLAZERS

---

1 Signed as a free agent after leaving his hometown Minnesota club, this fireman spent five seasons in Boston, setting the current club season mark for saves by a lefty with 24. Double.

2 In two full seasons with the Sox, this 6'5" flamethrower bagged 54 saves in 67 chances before moving to the Cards, where he set a new ML career save mark (since broken). Single.

3 Sparky Lyle was in the Sox pen when they won the flag in 1967. His five saves were runner-up for the club lead to what former Kansas City Athletic who nailed 20 of the club's total of 44 saves? Three-bagger.

4 Nine years after defeating the BoSox in a World Series game, he paced the Sox in saves with 20 despite not being acquired until July of that season. Even noting that Stan Belinda was second on the team with 10 still makes this a hard double.

5 He led the AL in saves with eight in 1909 and also won 16 games for the BoSox. He was coming off a rookie season that included a 1.82 ERA. His third and final season in the majors saw a rise in ERA to 2.88, hiking his career figure to 2.28. He currently stands eighth on the Sox' all-time career ERA list among hurlers in a minimum of 200 innings. Who is this all-too-fleeting Sox hurler? Three-run homer.

6 Joining the Sox after leading the AL in saves the previous year, he netted 32 saves in his first Beantown campaign. Dogged by knee injuries and a contentious relationship with Sox fans, this closer was finished in the Hub two years later. Single, plus a RBI for his fine initial season in Fenway.

7 Two years after going 12–9 as a regular in the Sox rotation, he set a record, later broken, for consecutive saves converted with 54 over two seasons. Leaving Fenway after Tommy John surgery, this curveballer proved he still had plenty left in his right arm. Single, plus a RBI for his two-year save streak.

8 What future 200-game winner led the AL with seven saves while sporting Sox garb in 1915? The clues are ample for those who know career patterns to collect a two-run double.

9 The pen was not the Sox' strong point when they copped the 1975 AL flag. What former Kansas City Royals starter led the club with just 15 saves? Two-run triple.

10 All five of the main starters on the 1912 World Champion Crimson Hose club also worked out of the pen. Which of the quintet led the club in relief appearances with 14 and also tied for the team lead in saves with a mere two? The previous year he had shared the AL lead in saves. Born Carlos Clolo, he played under a much more common name. Home run.

11 While other AL teams in the 1920s and 1930s began to realize the importance of relief specialists and developed bullpenners like Firpo Marberry and Johnny Murphy, the Red Sox lagged way behind. Prior to the emergence of Ellis Kinder in the early 1950s, who held the Sox career saves record with a meager total of 20? His season high of seven came in a year when he went 16–10 under player-manager Joe Cronin. Two-run double.

12 Not only is this chucker the first to appear in half of the Sox games in a season, but he's also the initial Fenway fireman to log 300 appearances from the pen without ever starting a game. RBI single.

13 Babe Ruth pitched in relief on occasion for the Sox. What other two members of the 500-homer club made solo relief appearances in crimson threads a year apart? Single for this Hall of Fame pair, plus a RBI for the two-year span in question.

14 Boston lost the 1948 flag to Cleveland in the first ever AL pennant playoff game. What lefty could not be faulted for the crushing loss, as he notched a dazzling 10–4 mark and a club-leading five saves? Bases loaded triple.

AB: 14
Hits: 14
Total Bases: 30
RBI: 17

INNING 5
GOLD GLOVE GOLIATHS

1 The only Sox pitcher to win bullion for his fielding was a master at varying speeds and threw what he dubbed a "foshball," a forkball-change combo that helped him bag 17 wins one year in Fenway flannels. He rates a single, plus a RBI for his golden year.

2 Prior to expansion, Bobby Doerr, not surprisingly, held the Sox record for the highest career FA (.980) by a second baseman in a minimum of 500 games at that position. We think it will surprise you enough to award a triple for the name of the Soxer whose .972 pre-expansion career mark at second ranked second to Doerr.

3 Give yourself a well-deserved double for pegging the first Sox receiver after Carlton Fisk to earn a Gold Glove. Tally a RBI for nailing the year he netted the honor.

4 Red Sox property for 10 consecutive seasons, he pitched in only eight of them owing to a career interruption. In four of the eight he fielded a perfect 1.000, helping him to set a Sox pre-expansion club record for the highest FA by a pitcher (.980) in a minimum of 200 games with the team. We'll add that he was a member of Ted Williams's only postseason unit and still award a three-bagger.

5 George Scott and Mo Vaughn currently rank first and second, respectively, in games played at first base for the Red Sox but only third and fourth, respectively, in career assists. What Hall of Famer ranks first with 614 assists in 807 games? Two-bagger.

6 He won a Sox club-record eight Gold Gloves in 10 years and might have strung together nine straight had a knee injury not shelved him for more than half the season the year after he nabbed his first award. Single.

7 Name the only Red Sox infielder to date that bagged three straight Gold Gloves. His reign was ended by a future Hall of Famer who won far more than three in a row. He's worth a deuce, and the Famer will bring an extra base.

8 Fourteen years had passed since a Gold Glove came the Sox' way when the man who holds the club's top two season FA marks at his position copped the award in his ninth year in crimson threads. Single, plus a RBI for the season he earned top fielding honors.

9 In his lone Sox season, he set the club mark for fewest errors (minimum 125 games) for a BoSox second sacker with just four. Yet he was deemed expendable even though he started for the AL at the keystone sack in that year's All-Star Game. Single, plus a RBI for the year.

10 What pastureman holds the Sox season mark for putouts and in the process set a new AL standard when he became the first ALer to log 500 putouts (503), a mark that stood until the White Sox' Chet Lemon snagged 512 in 1977? RBI single, plus an extra base for the year.

11 In 18 seasons of big league play with five clubs, this outfielder grabbed just one Gold Glove. It came with his first team, the BoSox, naturally. Despite his lean frame and solid speed, he lacked the range needed to be a top flychaser. Single, plus a RBI for his award-winning year.

12 In the lone season he played as many as 100 games with the Sox, he set the pre-expansion club record for the highest FA (.976) by a player in a minimum of 100 games at third base. The mark came in his 10th of 12 seasons in the majors, was later tied by Rico Petrocelli, and was then broken by a more recent Sox hot-corner operative. Our man finished his career with the 1960 Cubs and six years later was hired to pilot the Astros. He's worth a solo homer in his own right, plus two more RBI for the BoSox current season record holder for the highest FA by a third sacker.

13 Upon winning two straight Gold Gloves at one position in crimson garb, he was shifted by the Sox to another location for the next two seasons, only to return to his natural spot, where he bagged his third fielding honor in his first year back. Double, plus an extra base for nailing both positions.

14 Whose record did John Valentin break for the best career FA by a Sox shortstop in a minimum of 500 games at the position? His .971 career mark ranks only a point below Valentin's .972, but in many hitting departments he rates first among all shortstops in Sox history. RBI single.

AB: 14
Hits: 14
Total Bases: 28
RBI: 10

INNING 6
SHELL-SHOCKED SLINGERS

1 Five years after emerging as the Sox' ace, he posted the highest season ERA (5.61) among ML qualifiers while logging a dismal 9–13 slate. Already in his ninth campaign, he led many to believe his best days were well behind him. But he proved doubters enormously wrong, albeit elsewhere in the bigs. Single.

2 Prior to the season that Tim Wakefield surpassed him, the Sox' former all-time loss leader with 112 had long been a resident of the Hall of Fame. Just a single here.

3 Three hurlers were tagged for 100 or more HRs in Red Sox livery prior to AL expansion in 1961. The leader with 123 gave up his last dinger as a member of the 1963 Twins and never ceded more than 23 homers in a season. Triple.

4 While posting the highest season ERA (5.59) to date by a Sox pitcher in a minimum of 200 innings, he also averaged the most base runners per nine (14.94) among BoSoxers who logged at least that many frames. Like many of the men encountered in this chapter, this 5'9" righty was solid during numerous other campaigns. Single, plus a RBI for his singularly awful year.

5 In 1925 the Sox for the first time had a qualifier with an ERA over 5.00. In fact, they had two chuckers with 5.00+ ERAs in a minimum of 154 innings. Name both for a three-run homer, down to a two-bagger for just one.

6 What Soxer holds the club record for homers surrendered (32) during a 20-win season? Along the way, he failed to throw a single shutout in over 270 innings but still posted an ERA nearly half a run below the league average that year. Single, plus a RBI for the year this hurler logged these contradictory stats.

7 When he surrendered 10 taters in 1901, he set a Boston AL mark that would last until 1929. But the 172 total runs and 48 unearned runs he surrendered in 1901 have never been surpassed in club annals. Who is he for a RBI triple?

8 In 1956 he went 3–12 with a 5.14 ERA and became the first Soxer to surrender at least 20 homers in a season in fewer than 150 innings when he yielded 21 bombs in only 126 frames. Believe it or not, this Virginian had paced the AL with 22 victories as a member of another club just three years earlier. Mama named him Erwin, but no one called him that in the bigs. RBI double.

9 After an excellent rookie year in 1924 that included a 3.47 ERA, what southpaw gave up 86 runs in 1925 in just 94⅓ innings in the course of going 3–8? In his final starting appearance in 1926, he was pulled in the third inning after giving up seven runs. Grand-slam homer.

10 Although this chucker never quite knew where his pitches were going, batters did when they tagged him for a Sox team-record 38 homers one season. He is currently the lone hurler to suffer double-digit season loss totals as many as eight times with the BoSox. Single.

11 The Red Sox previous season record holder for taters yielded still holds the club mark for fewest career wins (56) by a Sox chucker who surrendered at least 100 round-trippers. No meatball, he later shared the AL lead in victories the year after the BoSox dealt him. RBI single.

12 Who holds the Sox club season record for wins among hurlers that posted an ERA of at least 5.00? Although he bagged a team-leading 16 victories, he failed to complete any of his 33 starts and yielded 36 homers. Single, plus a RBI for the year.

13 Who was the only Boston AL slab man to suffer a 20-loss season despite having Babe Ruth as part of his supporting cast? Would you believe he'd earlier led the AL in winning percentage with Ruth's bat as his chief offensive weapon? RBI double.

14 The last time two BoSoxers shared the AL season loss leadership, each of them dropped 18 for a Beantown squad that lost 100 games. Triple for naming this oft-defeated pair, plus a RBI for the year. Single for anything less.

AB: 14
Hits: 14
Total Bases: 28
RBI: 15

INNING 7
HEROES AND GOATS

1 What infamous Sox goat first donned the horns 12 years earlier with the Dodgers when he got nailed at third while attempting to stretch a misplayed ball in the fifth and final game of that season's World Series? Single.

2 Can a player be deemed a Series hero for hitting .250, scoring only two runs, and bagging just one RBI? The Sox had just such an idol in 1918 when a certain rookie gardener picked precisely the right moments to shine with both his bat and glove in fall play. Name this obscure frosh and score a two-run triple.

3 Beantowners cheered when his groundout made Boston the world champs and then booed him a year later when he hit .276 as the Sox regular in the number two slot in the order. Bad hop single.

4 Johnny Pesky, perhaps unfairly, was made the goat of the 1946 World Series when Enos Slaughter scored from first base on what should have been no more than a long single. Who was the weak-armed outfielder whose less than stellar relay throw led to Pesky's legendary slight hesitation? Triple.

5 Bone chips in his throwing arm helped this gloved goat commit the most errors in a season (43) of any third baseman since Ted Williams's bush league days. In fact, this hot-corner horror is the last AL regular to field below .900. Single for him, plus a RBI for the year.

6 What chucker went from goat to hero in a 24-hour period when he was knocked out of the box after one inning during an 11–4 loss that knotted a certain World Series 3–3, only to return the following afternoon to win the Series clincher in relief? RBI single for him, extra base for the year it occurred.

7 What hero once hit two homers in a game into the rightfield stands in Gavy Cravath's home park that were shortened that fall to accommodate more spectators in leading the Sox to a 5–4 Series-clinching win against Cravath's Phils? Triple, plus a RBI for the year.

8 Was he the goat here or was it manager Joe McCarthy? In any case, no good explanation has ever surfaced for why this right-hander started the 1948 pennant playoff game against the Indians. Deepening the puzzle is our retrospective knowledge that after the Tribe blasted him that day, he never again started a game in the majors. RBI triple.

9 The Red Sox thought they had the right man at the plate with two out in the top of the ninth of the 1949 season finale at Yankee Stadium, but Sox faithful groaned when he fouled out to Yogi Berra to end all hope in Boston. Generous two-bagger.

10 He trotted home from third base on Jack Chesbro's wild pitch with two out in the ninth inning to bring Boston the AL pennant on the closing day of the 1904 season. Embraced as a hero by Hub denizens, he would score only one more run in a ML uniform after that day. Take a sweet swing at this one and garner a RBI double.

11 Although this Sox starter failed to hold the lead in a memorable Game 7 of a World Series, don't paste horns on him, since the Mets scored just twice in 17 innings during his two earlier Series victories. RBI single.

12 Bill Lee started the seventh game of the 1975 Series, but it was this rookie reliever who earned the loss and went on to appear in just one more regular season game two years later with Boston before departing for good. It's been a while, so we'll upgrade him to a double.

13 What 2,000-hit man did little to aid Boston in the 1975 Series, stroking just one hit in 19 at bats (.053)? A year later he flew Fenway's coop but can now land in your nest for a double.

AB: 13
Hits: 13
Total Bases: 26
RBI: 8

INNING 8
RED-HOT ROOKIES

1 The first rookie middle infielder ever to blast 30 homers wore Sox raiment that season. Stop at first, but tally a RBI for the year.

2 Nineteen wins as a rookie with a last-place team generally portends some big years ahead. But our man finished with just 42 victories, all with the Crimson Hose. His last came less than nine months before he died from stab wounds he received in a brawl during a fish fry in his honor in the spring of 1932. Name him for a two-run triple.

3 Summoned at long last to the show after belting .300+ in each of his last five seasons in the Sox' minor league chain, he proved he belonged by stroking .349 in 381 plate appearances as a Fenway freshman. We'll close our eyes and let you dribble a single past the mound.

4 What Boston infielder led all AL rookies in triples in 1901 with 15? Two years later he tagged nine home runs to set a club mark for the most dingers by a second sacker that would last until 1937. Solo homer.

5 He shared the AL triples crown with nine as a Sox frosh, rare for a player at his position. Never again did he lead in that category during the four decades in which he appeared up top. Shouldn't need more to rap a single here, plus a RBI for the year.

6 Although he led AL rookies in doubles, runs, and walks despite missing over 50 games, this Sox shortstop finished a distant third in that season's rookie balloting. RBI single, plus an extra base for the year.

7 What Sox Rookie of the Year recipient won only 24 career games in Beantown? Knowing that he narrowly defeated the A's Dick Howser by one vote in that year's freshman balloting reduces this to a RBI single.

8 In 1952 and 1953 the Red Sox underwent a massive youth movement, hoping to resuscitate a rapidly declining team. Of the many rookies that debuted in Crimson Hose in those two seasons, only one was still active in the majors the year that the New York Mets amazed the baseball world and won it all. The clue that he appeared against the Mets in their first season as an expansion team and finished with Houston, their co-expansion club, should get the savvy home for a RBI triple.

9 In 1901 he singled and stole a base in his lone at bat; in 1902 he tied for the AL rookie lead with two home runs; in 1903 he was the only man to play for the first Boston AL flag winner who had a brother also playing in the majors that year. He made only 206 career hits, but his brother rapped close to 2,000. The family name alone will bring three bases, plus two RBI for his first name.

10 Not only did he cop AL Rookie of the Year honors, but this outfielder also set the junior-loop freshman mark with a circuit-topping 47 doubles. The owner of solid stats across the board, he also led the AL in runs and slugging. Single, plus a RBI for the year.

11 In 1938 this Soxer led ML rooks with 15 wins but slipped the next two seasons before moving to his native city of Cleveland, where he had his best years. Back with the Sox in 1946, he won seven games and made three relief outings in the Series against the Cards. RBI double.

12 After tryouts in the Sox pasture, he shined in his first full season, rapping .287 and leading AL gateway guardians in assists. A .295 follow-up showed promise of better things to come until a car accident shelved him for the entire season. Never the same upon returning, he played just one more season in Beantown before exiting the big league stage at age 28. RBI single, plus an extra ribby for his initial year as a regular.

13 Named Minor League Player of the Year after capturing the International League's Triple Crown with Pawtucket, this frosh slugger plated 102 runs for the Sox a year later despite missing 18 games. In addition, he became the first AL frosh ever to bat .300 while fanning as many as 100 times. Single, plus a RBI for his stellar rookie campaign.

14 A certain Sox switch-hitter paced AL rookies in games, at bats, doubles, homers, RBI, and stolen bases but failed to win top freshman honors. However, this outfielder did earn the only vote awarded to an AL yearling that season that did not go to the winner, as everyone was snowed under by a frosh who later made Cooperstown. Double, but you need both red-hot rookie names to score here, plus a RBI for the year.

AB: 14
Hits: 14
Total Bases: 26
RBI: 16

INNING 9
PEERLESS PILOTS

1 Who is the lone BoSox pilot to finish second in the AL twice by just a one-game margin? Single, plus a ribby if you know both years he fell short by so narrow a margin.

2 Who is the most recent man to manage the Sox after winning a pennant earlier as a player-manager? Triple, plus a RBI for his flag winner.

3 What flag-winning Red Sox skipper played on two Series-bound Yankees teams? True, this backup backstop logged only 26 career contests in pinstripes, but he played with six clubs in just six seasons and even appeared in two Series games for the Reds *against* the Bombers. A former Pawtucket pilot, he's good for a RBI single.

4 Who was the last pilot to write Ted Williams's name on a lineup card? Two-run single.

5 It's gift time! What Sox field boss previously managed Michael Jordan in 1994 with the Birmingham Barons of the Southern League? Baltimore chop single.

6 Who was the only BoSox flag-winning skipper never to play in the majors and who has yet to make the Hall of Fame? A minor league catcher, he later roamed the bigs managing six clubs, including an ill-fated Sox Series entrant. Double.

7 Roger Clemens's first big league skipper went 312–282 in four seasons at Fenway and exited after the Rocket's frosh campaign with over 1,600 career managerial wins. Name him for a single.

8 Who was the first man to catch in the majors and later pilot the Sox to two consecutive last-place finishes? Two-run double.

9 No skipper since Joe McCarthy in 1946 has guided the Sox to more victories in a season than this man, who came within a game of taking the Sox much farther. Single, plus a RBI for the year.

10 What 10-year infielder closed his career with the Sox and later managed them for four seasons, finishing above .500 in each campaign? Some thought this bespectacled pilot resembled a college professor, so avoid flunking his course and stroke a RBI double.

11 Who replaced Joe McCarthy at the Red Sox helm? Earlier, he guided a rival AL outfit to the Series, but no such magic came his way during his two-year Fenway stay. A former catcher for another Series-bound club, he's worth a double, but you can notch an extra base apiece for knowing both the flag winner he guided and the one on which he played in October.

12 Only one field general guided Boston clubs in the AL and the NL. The 1909 Sox finished third with 88 wins in his lone full year in their driver's seat, but he crashed in his only season with the Boston Nationals, placing dead last with 100 losses. Knock this one over the fence with three ducks on the pond or you'll be soaking wet.

13 What former reliever for Earl Weaver became the first Red Sox pitching coach to manage the Crimson Hose? Single, plus a ribby for the year.

14 Who piloted BoSox teams to consecutive fourth-place finishes in an eight-team league while losing 69 games the first year with a highly respectable .548 winning percentage and then triumphed in only 69 contests the next campaign for a .448 winning percentage, the lowest in ML history by a first-division club? Triple.

AB: 14
Hits: 14
Total Bases: 26
RBI: 14

GAME 7

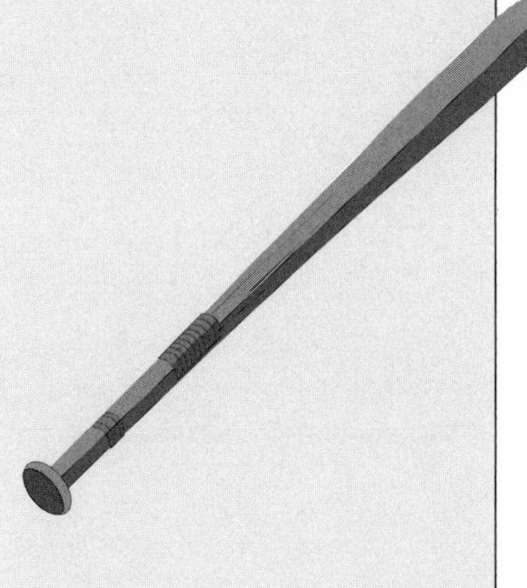

INNING 1
RBI RULERS

1 In his initial year with the Sox, he became the first batsman to lead them in RBI without ever taking the field defensively when he plated 87 mates despite missing some 20 games. Bombarded by injuries again the following season, this fading 18-year vet exited the majors. RBI single, plus an extra base for his leadership year.

2 The Sox are the only team in ML history to sport two middle infielders that each totaled 100 or more RBI three years in a row. You need the duo and their three-year 100 RBI span to score a double.

3 Not since the Deadball Era had a Soxer posted fewer RBI in a season (minimum 150 games) than a certain rookie shortstop plating just 29 mates while slugging only .316 with a mere 17 extra base hits in 480 plate appearances. Never again a regular, he finished with the 1988 Phils. Two bases for this Colombian native, plus a RBI for the year.

4 The Sox had four 100 RBI men in 1940 and five who clouted 20 or more homers. Which one of their 20-tater quintet did not also bag 100 RBI? RBI double.

5 Who posted the most RBI in a season without either leading or sharing the Sox team high? The club leader also topped the AL that year, and these two combined to punish opposing pitchers with 292 ribbies—the most since expansion by a pair of teammates. Single for our runner-up and a RBI for the league leader, plus an extra base for the year.

6 What former three-time AL ribby king racked up a team-leading 99 RBI with just five home runs in 1924, his only full season with the Red Sox? RBI double.

7 Name the Sox stickman who hit the fewest homers since WWII while having a 100 RBI season. He clocked 15 circuit blasts and pushed across 103 runners, 16 more than Ted Williams that campaign. Double, plus a RBI for the year.

8 In 1923, with the Lively Ball Era in full sway, this gateway guardian led the Sox with a lowly 82 RBI and also topped the club in runs with 91. Previously, he had seen fall action in 1920 with Cleveland and later did likewise with the 1929 A's. He at one time held the ML season record for doubles and shared the same first and last name as a NL outfielder whose career overlapped his own. Two-baser.

9 In his only full season with the Sox, this Hall of Famer paced the club with 73 RBI and a .866 OPS despite missing 20 games. He finished his career with Baltimore in 1957 by stroking .297 in 99 games and is good for two bases, plus a RBI for his leadership campaign.

10 Who was the first rookie to lead the Red Sox in RBI? It was a sign of good things to come. One base for him, a ribby for the year.

11 Who played the fewest games in a season among Soxers with 100+ RBI? Missing over 40 contests, he still plated 107 ribbies, a figure falling 58 below his career-best total set with another AL club. Single.

12 Who totaled the fewest career RBI among players that plated 100 runs at least once in Sox garb? Last seen with the 1933 Pale Hose, he racked up 103 RBI two years earlier while patrolling Fenway's garden but is far better known for another batting achievement in Crimson Hose. Triple.

13 Slam a two-run shot into the centerfield bleachers by identifying the right fielder who paced the weak-hitting 1908 AL Hub edition with a meager 63 RBI and also set the record that season for the lowest OBP (.394) by a junior-loop OBP leader. Those who don't know their Deadball Sox stars will need to call their general practitioner for some extra stimulants in order to score here.

14 When Ted Williams drove in his 236th run, he broke the team mark for ribbies by a performer who spent his entire career with the Red Sox. Naturally we're looking for the previous record holder whose contributions to the Crimson Hose were far greater in another capacity. A rough customer, he's worth a three-run homer.

AB: 14
Hits: 14
Total Bases: 31
RBI: 13

INNING 2
MVP MARVELS

1 We can't offer more than a scratch hit for the first freshman to win MVP, but we'll add a gift RBI for pegging the year a BoSox rook pulled off this super first.

2 Sox great Bobby Doerr's highest MVP finish was third. What year did it occur? RBI double.

3 What two BoSox pitchers finished fourth and fifth, respectively, in the MVP balloting one season and what year was it? You need all three answers to score a two-run double.

4 What year did Ted Williams finish second by just one vote in the closest MVP balloting in AL history? Single, plus a RBI for the player who beat him out.

5 What Hub performer placed third in the AL MVP race in the only season during his nine big league campaigns that he ever earned a vote? Learning that he did it the season after the Sox won their first flag in 21 years reduces this to a single.

6 Between 1959 and 1966, only one Crimson Hose member cracked the top five in the AL MVP race, and at that he placed exactly fifth, albeit just one vote behind the Twins' Harmon Killebrew. Easy to misstep here so we'll ante two.

7 The first Soxer since Teddy Ballgame to crack the AL's MVP top five for four years running also paced the junior circuit in homers and RBI in one of those seasons but failed to earn a single first-place vote. Single.

8 Who played the most career games in Sox threads without ever winning MVP? During his lengthy Beantown tenure, he placed in the top 10 four times and once reached as high as third. RBI single.

9 When Ted Williams won his final bat title, he finished just seventh in the MVP balloting, in part because most of the Hub votes went elsewhere. What BoSoxer won the MVP Award and what year are we talking about? You need both for a double.

10 What Sox slugger copped MVP the year he also became the first player ever to lead the AL outright in both homers and triples? Single, plus a RBI for the season.

11 You'd hoot us out of Fenway if we offered more than a bunt single for naming the Sox MVP recipient who that season also became the most recent batter to cop a Triple Crown. We'll place a ribbon on this gift by adding a RBI for the year.

12 When this Sox bopper bagged the MVP, he also became the first ALer to fan 150 times in a season in which he batted .300. Interestingly, he repeated this dubious batting feat in each of the next two seasons. Single, plus a RBI for the year.

13 What Sox MVP honoree turned 24 in August of his triumphant season but never grabbed another such trophy even though he played well into his forties. Historically, performers at his position find it all but impossible to repeat, let alone win even once. Single, plus a RBI for the year.

14 Naming the only BoSox reliever other than Ellis Kinder to earn MVP votes before the expansion era may tax even the most die-hard Sox devotee, so we'll share that he appeared in 70 games, going 10–5 with 14 saves for a forlorn Crimson Hose crew that placed seventh in an eight-club league. Two-run double, plus an extra base for the year.

AB: 14
Hits: 14
Total Bases: 20
RBI: 12

INNING 3
TUMULTUOUS TRADES

1 You knew this one was coming, so let's get it over and done with. On March 22, 1972, the Yanks and Sox engaged in a straight-up swap so infamous in Boston that you'll need to name *both* players just to reach first safely.

2 Owner Tom Yawkey showed his commitment to improving the Sox in his very first year of stewardship when he jettisoned mediocre hurler Bob Kline, anemic stick Rabbit Warstler, and 125 grand for three key members of Connie Mack's 1929–1931 AL dynasty. Triple for all three, single for anything less.

3 Yawkey continued wheeling and dealing the following campaign, tossing $25,000 to Cleveland, along with Bob Weiland and Bob Seeds for Dick Porter and a supposedly sore-armed hurler who proved to be a future two-time 20-game winner with the Sox. RBI single.

4 Heathcliff Slocumb was all Boston needed in 1997 to pry two players from the Mariners who were key performers on the

Sox 2004 champs. Grab a double for nailing both but zip for anything less.

5 The Sox emptied their pockets on October 26, 1934, to acquire this future Cooperstown inductee from Washington for shortstop Lyn Lary, plus a cool 225 gees. RBI single.

6 Sure, George Scott produced fairly well during his first year back with Boston in 1977, but the performer the Sox squandered even up for Scott would hit .302 and stroke 201 homers after exiting Fenway. RBI single.

7 Although Mike Boddicker made valuable contributions to Boston, the pair the Sox dealt to Baltimore in exchange for his services would eventually blossom into All-Stars. Although neither was an overnight success, we still can't offer more than a single base for each.

8 What pair of hurlers did the Sox deal to the Expos in exchange for Pedro Martinez? One was the son of a former Sox homer champ, the other went 18–8 for another NL outfit in 2004 before returning to the AL. Single, but you need both to score.

9 One of the forgotten swindles the Bombers perpetrated against the Sox occurred in the winter of 1923 when the Yanks shipped catcher Al DeVormer in exchange for outfielder Harvey Hendrick and an Iowa-born righty who would win at least 15 games five times in pinstripes, including an AL-leading 24 in 1928. RBI double.

10 Christmas came early on December 18, 1918, when the Sox gift wrapped a controversial performer who became the only man ever to win 25 or more games in a season twice for the Bombers in exchange for chuckers Allan Russell and Bob McGraw and 40 grand. Name him for a deuce.

11 On November 17, 1947, the BoSox tossed over 300 grand plus six players to the St. Louis Browns for a performer who would produce a ton of runs in Beantown and a key righty on their 1948 near pennant winner. Triple for the pair, single for one.

12 In another Yankees mega-duping, the Sox obtained Muddy Ruel, Del Pratt, Sammy Vick, and Hank Thormahlen for four players. One of the quartet went to Cooperstown, and another would bat over .300 as a regular on the Bombers' first two flag winners. Homer for both, two bases for just one.

13 On May 2, 1927, the Sox fleeced a certain future star second sacker from Washington, only to foolishly return him to the nation's capital in the winter of 1928 for Milt Gaston, Hod Lisenbee, Bobby Reeves, and two others. RBI double.

14 Mickey McDermott had already seen his best years and outfielder Tom Umphlett proved a major disappointment after the BoSox dumped them on Washington in exchange for what future Hub standout? RBI single.

AB: 14
Hits: 14
Total Bases: 26
RBI: 7

INNING 4
WHO'D THEY COME UP WITH?

You'll need the name of another major league team here, and the year each of these BoSox stalwarts first appeared in the majors will earn two extra RBI.

1 Jackie Jensen. RBI single.

2 Keith Foulke. Double.

3 Jimmy Collins. Double.

4 David Ortiz. Bloop single.

5 Troy O'Leary. RBI single.

6 Lou Criger. Triple.

7 Herb Pennock. Double.

8 Tim Wakefield. Single.

9 Ernie Shore. Grand slammer.

10 Bill Campbell. RBI single.

11 Heinie Wagner. Two-run homer.

12 Rich Garces. Double.

13 Doug Mirabelli. RBI single.

14 Jesse Burkett. Three-run homer.

15 Mike Torrez. RBI single.

AB: 15
Hits: 15
Total Bases: 30
RBI: 34

INNING 5
STRIKEOUT KINGS

1 After Cy Young led the AL in Ks in its inaugural season, the BoSox suffered a long dry spell before they produced their second whiff leader. Who was the next AL Hub hurler to win or share junior-loop strikeout honors? Home run.

2 Who was the first twirler, other than Cy Young, to register as many as 200 Ks in a season with Boston in the AL? RBI single, plus an extra base for the year he did it.

3 Who was the first Red Sox ERA qualifier to fan more than one batter per nine innings in a season? Single, plus a RBI for the year.

4 In 1948 the Sox lost the pennant in a one-game playoff. Name the lone Sox hurler that year who bagged as many as 100 Ks. In a down year throughout the AL for whiffs, his total of 116 was only 48 behind the loop leader, Bob Feller. Triple.

5 Who paced the AL in Ks during his only year in crimson threads? Knowing this chucker's 220 whiffs were fewer than he fanned in each of his first three ML seasons lowers this to a RBI single, especially after we note that he also led the Sox hill staff in wins and innings pitched, with 13 and 198, respectively.

6 In the decade 1931–1940, who was the only Sox hurler to notch as many as 150 Ks in a season? The owner of three of the club's top five strikeout seasons during that 10-year span, he merits a double, plus a RBI for the year he racked up 153 whiffs.

7 What Red Sox slab man closed one season by fanning at least 10 batters in each of his last eight starts? Interestingly, he stretched that streak to 10 starts over two years (excluding a relief appearance), and during his record-setting run he went 8–1 for the Sox with 130 Ks while walking just 11. Single.

8 In 1927 what hurler led the Sox with 21 losses and tied for the club lead in Ks with a meager total of 77? Homer, plus two additional RBI for the Sox arm that tied him for the lead.

9 Who became the first Sox tosser since World War II to lead the AL in whiffs? Despite toiling for 15 years with three clubs, this righty never again came within 100 Ks of his league-leading total of 246. Single, plus an extra base for the year.

10 In 1957 what hurler set a BoSox pre-expansion record for the most Ks in fewer than 100 innings when he fanned 62 hitters in just 94 frames? Home run even after we add that he also paced the club in saves.

11 A routine single is yours for the name of the only hurler to notch as many as 1,000 Ks in Boston AL garb prior to AL expansion in 1961.

12 Prior to expansion, what Soxer held the club season mark for strikeouts by a southpaw? It's not Babe Ruth, but the lefty you're after also went by a famous moniker, perhaps because his given name was Hubert. Triple, plus a RBI for the year.

13 No Sox southpaw has ever posted a 200-K season, but this lefty holds the club's top two season highs. Once the team's number two man in the rotation, he retired with more career wins than any other player to date born in Utah. RBI single.

14 The first Sox hurler (minimum 150 innings) to average more than a K per nine frames in a season also set a whiff mark that year that may never be surpassed. Known for his deadly sidearm heater, he was one of the most intimidating mound specimens of his era. RBI single, plus an extra base for knowing his record.

AB: 14
Hits: 14
Total Bases: 31
RBI: 13

INNING 6
STELLAR STICKWIELDERS

1 Between 1963 and 1968, Yaz led all Sox regulars in batting in every year but one. Right, we're looking for the performer who slipped in during Yaz's reign, and later snuck into two Series games for the Cards *against* the Sox in 1967. But we'll wager a three-run homer that your answer here will be wrong.

2 The Sox featured many of the sweetest-swinging pitchers in baseball history, but just one ever stroked five hits in a game. Knowing that he did it for a Crimson Hose world champ and that we're only offering a single should make this one a snap.

3 During his ML record-tying stretch of seven straight 40-double seasons, this Soxer topped the AL twice in that department, including a high of 51. Just a single for this two-bag titan.

4 It's difficult to lead the league in both hits and walks, since patient batters exchange potential hits for free passes while others shun walks and accumulate hits. The only player to lead the AL in both categories in the same season did it with the Crimson Hose, slapping 183 hits while drawing 95 walks. Double, plus a RBI for the year.

5 When this Sox slugger collected over 400 total bases, he became the first to do so in the AL in 41 years. Single for him, but you snag two extra bases for the previous junior-circuit performer to turn the trick.

6 In each of his four seasons in Fenway, he scored over 100 runs, with a high of 123. Never a league leader in Boston, he did top the junior circuit with 136 runs two years before donning Crimson Hose. Single.

7 Who posted the lowest season BA ever by a BoSox batting-title qualifier (minimum 502 plate appearances)? A member of Ralph Houk's crew, he also posted the lowest season OPS by a Sox qualifier that met the above criteria since the aught years. A meager .262 OBA coupled with a paltry .311 SA sank his OPS to .573, the worst among all qualifiers that year in both leagues. RBI triple.

8 Who holds the Red Sox record for career singles? No great challenge here if you just go for the obvious answer. Single.

9 In his 10 full or partial seasons with Boston, his best campaign came when he cracked the AL's top five in OPS (.975) and slugging (.578). Injuries dogged this former Sox first-round draft pick just when he seemed to be putting it all together. Single, plus a RBI for his finest season.

10 Since the Deadball Era, who posted the lowest OBP among Soxers with at least 4,000 plate appearances? All but the last of this slick fielder's 12 seasons were spent in Fenway, and his .317

OBP with Boston is even lower than that of light-hitting Rick Burleson. No middle infielder, he actually had more pop in his prime than any other ALer at his position. Double.

11 Subsequent to his rookie season, Wade Boggs paced all Sox qualifiers in BA every year with the exception of his last in Fenway. The outfielder who ended Boggs's skein hit just .266 that year, two years after Boston acquired him for Lee Smith. RBI triple.

12 What outfielder who was approaching age 39 led the AL in OPS for the first and only time in his career in his first year in Red Sox garb? Two bases for him, plus a RBI for his big year.

13 Excepting players already enshrined in Cooperstown, who rapped the most career hits for the BoSox among retired performers boasting a .300 career BA in Sox threads? One of their top strokers for a while, he left the game with a .303 average on 1,400 hits, all of it compiled in the Hub. RBI single.

14 Three Soxers have slugged over .600 in a season without drilling at least 30 homers. The Babe was the first and Teddy Ballgame did it five times. Who was the third? Grab a single, plus a RBI for the year.

AB: 14
Hits: 14
Total Bases: 26
RBI: 10

INNING 7
HOME RUN KINGS

1 Lou Clinton went to the Angels in exchange for this first sacker who finished second on the 1965 Sox with 22 seat-reachers before exiting Boston himself when George Scott was found waiting in the wings. Arguably one of the least remembered players to slug 100+ homers during the 1960s, his name's worth a line-shot double.

2 What year did Babe Ruth either win or share the AL home run crown for the first time? RBI single.

3 He poked a ML-leading 43 homers with the Sox but dipped to 23 and then 11 before moving to the Angels, where he never recovered his power stroke. RBI single, plus an extra base for his leadership year.

4 Just once in 19 seasons of patrolling Fenway's pasture did he top the AL in homers, and even then our performer had to share the honor with three others. Single for him, a RBI for the year, plus an extra base for each man with whom he tied.

5 The first Boston AL rapper to post double-figure home run totals three years in a row was also the initial junior-circuit performer to accomplish this feat. He's going for a double, plus a RBI for his three-year span.

6 Who holds the Sox season record for grand slammers? Odds would favor a high homer total, but this slugger actually pounded less than 30 that year and never played for the Sox thereafter. Piece the clues together for a double, plus a RBI for the year.

7 Bobby Doerr leads all Sox second sackers in career home runs by a huge margin. The only other Sox second baseman to rip as many as 20 career home runs prior to AL expansion in 1961 slapped 34 round-trippers, and it was his club record that Doerr broke. Rates a RBI triple.

8 Signed out of high school, this Bonus Baby, at age 17, became the youngest man to date ever to play for the Sox. At one time Boston's season record holder for homers by a catcher, he later set the Pirates' club receivers' mark as well, and three years hence caught a perfect game with yet a third team. Double for him; the team and pitcher for whom he called the perfecto is worth a RBI.

9 What BoSoxer was the first slugger to lead the AL in dingers while serving primarily as a DH? Single, plus a RBI for the year.

10 Ted Williams cranked 29 homers in 1960, his final season, in just 390 plate appearances. Only one other Sox slugger to date has belted 20 or more homers in a season in fewer than 400 PA. Take the clue that all of his circuit blasts that year came prior to August 15 and streak to a RBI double.

11 In 1902 what Sox first sacker bagged six taters to set the club mark for the most home runs by a switch-hitter that would later be tied twice but was not broken until 1967? Triple.

12 His 18 jacks in 1932 were the most by a BoSoxer between 1920 and 1935. RBI triple.

13 The first right-handed batter to top the AL in dingers wearing a Boston uniform went homerless in his only Series with the Sox two years later. Enough clues there to triple, but it's down to a double if you don't also know the year he led.

14 In 1919 Babe Ruth hit a loop-leading 29 homers. Following his departure, the Sox hit just 20 jacks the next year as a *team.* Who led the 1920 club with seven, his personal season high to that point, although he would surpass it in each of his next four seasons? Take two for this 2,000-hit man who compiled just a .387 career slugging average.

AB: 14
Hits: 14
Total Bases: 31
RBI: 10

INNING 8
MASTER MOUNDSMEN

1 Twenty years after logging a 20–8 season in Boston, he made 50 relief outings for the BoSox before bidding the big leagues *adieu.* This veteran had way too much success elsewhere for us to ante more than a single.

2 Tally a single in your column for knowing the only man since Cy Young to toe the rubber in Sox flannels *after* collecting his 300th win with another club.

3 Following a 90-year drought since the last Soxer had won 20 games while walking fewer than 40 batters, it then happened twice in five seasons. We'll ante a single, but you need both recent control aces to score here.

4 Who is the only Soxer to relieve in over 30 games and start more than 20 contests in the same season? Two years later he set the club mark (later broken) for appearances in a season with 80. Well traveled, he tooled around with nine teams in 15 campaigns under the big top. RBI single, plus an extra base for the year.

5 The most recent pitcher to defeat the Yanks five times in a season bagged 22 victories that campaign for the Sox and later won 13 games one year in pinstripes. You should rap a single here, plus a RBI for the year he dominated the Bombers.

6 Only one Soxer has ever worked 300+ innings in a season without yielding a homer. Obviously a Deadballer, he did, however, surrender an inside-the-park job that year to Brooklyn's Hy Myers in his first inning ever of World Series mound action. Clues are there to help narrow this one to a double.

7 Other than Cy Young, who was the only Sox stalwart to bag more than 15 victories in a season at age 40 or older? Single, plus a RBI for the year.

8 In eight seasons with the Sox, he fashioned a modest 60–56 slate. However, 43 of those victories came over a three-year stretch when he shared the club lead with 12 and then paced the team with 15. The next season this Southern slinger bagged 16 for a Sox flag winner before his career abruptly nosedived. RBI single.

9 Who was the first post-WWII Red Sox twirler (minimum one inning pitched per team game played) to log two consecutive seasons with ERAs below 3.00? He just made it, too, with identical 2.99 figures in both years. Double.

10 What vastly underrated hurler went 13–11 for the 1906 Sox cellar club that was 36–94 on days when he didn't take the hill? Clues are right for a two-run triple.

11 Just one example of how much the 1967 Sox improved over the previous year can be found in their 1966 wins leader, who bagged all of 12. Although he notched 12 more for the flag winners, his total fell 10 behind club leader Jim Lonborg. Name him for a RBI double.

12 The only Soxer both to win and lose 20 in the same season went 21–21 for a team that was destined to win the pennant the following year. Who was he and what year did he do it? Triple if you know both parts, zero for less.

13 In his final season with the BoSox, a certain 200-game winner posted 23 victories to set a club record for the most wins with fewer than 100 strikeouts as he K'd a mere 98. At that, it was his career high in whiffs. Two years later, he won 21 for a Yankees flag winner while fanning just 68 hitters. Take those clues and romp to a double.

14 Cy Young and Babe Ruth share the record for the most starts in a season (41) for a BoSox pennant winner. Who stands third on this select list, two behind Young and Ruth with 39? We'll award a two-run double.

15 Just once have the Red Sox sported the lone 20-game winner in the majors, and this Texas-born tosser's name will send you to first.

AB: 15
Hits: 15
Total Bases: 25
RBI: 9

INNING 9
FALL CLASSICS

1 All eight Boston regulars played every inning in the field in the eight-game World Series affair in 1903. Name the only member of the eight who was no longer a regular on the repeat 1904 Boston pennant winner for a triple; also name his replacement and earn three RBI.

2 Name the 35-year-old second sacker who played every inning for Boston in the 1918 World Series after posting career regular-season highs in runs, BA, OBP, and SA. Earlier in his ML labors he played with the Braves, making him the first middle infielder to see regular duty with both Boston ML clubs. Born in Arlington, Mass., he died in Boston and rates a home run.

3 The Sox used 23 men in the 1975 World Series. What backup to Carlton Fisk caught 57 games in the regular season but rode the wood for the entire Series and the ALCS as well when Fisk caught every inning for the Sox in postseason play that year? A switch-hitter, he saw regular duty only in 1980, when he caught 103 games for the Cubs but nevertheless fashioned a 10-year career in the show. Three-run homer.

4 It shouldn't take you more than a few seconds to remember the only other Soxer besides Yaz to play in both the 1967 and 1975 Series. Single.

5 The first Crimson Hose member to bat as a DH in a Fall Classic debuted 16 years earlier with another AL outfit, but his DH appearance was his first taste of World Series action. Already 37, this barrel-chested Texan went on to play in the next two Series, representing a different club each time. RBI single.

6 Boston fans fondly recall Jim Lonborg's two masterful victories during the 1967 Series against the Cards. But can you recollect the reliever, who bagged 10 wins during the regular season and the only other triumph for Beantown in that clash? RBI double.

7 What Boston unit won a World Series despite a postseason .186 team BA and a .233 slugging average? Just a single, because there aren't that many Sox teams from which to choose.

8 Dick Williams used a teenaged lefty twice in relief against the Cards in 1967, making this Brooklyn boy the youngest pitcher ever in Series play. Take two for this fuzzy-cheeked chucker.

9 Although he toiled for parts of seven campaigns during the 1980s in Fenway, this righty reliever tends to slip through the cracks, even among avid Sox fans. In 1986, he wedged in the Mets' craw by winning Game 2 after failing to garner a single victory during the regular season that year. Tough enough for a two-run double.

10 Quick now, who was the only man to play for the Sox in both the 1975 and 1986 Series? RBI single.

11 The most recent Soxer to toss a complete-game shutout in fall action is also the most recent pitcher to start three of the first six games in a World Series. RBI single for this workhorse.

12 Although he earned just six career victories with the Sox, this 6'4" Connecticut hill topper started a World Series contest for the Crimson Hose. An 18-game winner a year earlier with Toronto of the International League, he played for the same skipper who tapped him the following year for Game 6 of that Fall Classic. It was this tosser's lone moment in the sun as he drifted ignominiously to the Cards, Expos, Yanks, and A's. Double.

13 Another surprise Sox Series starter, he posted a hefty 5.38 ERA during the regular season with a 10–12 ledger for a BoSox club that won 95 games. Of course he lost his Series start and posted a 7.11 ERA across two outings in that postseason clash. Double.

14 Just one pitcher since 1900 has batted anywhere other than ninth in a World Series starting lineup, and this stickman occupied the sixth slot. Shouldn't take you long to figure out who it was, so the chucker's a single. But we'll add two bases if you know his battery mate that day who hit last.

15 Elston Howard nearly could boast that he was the only ML performer who both won an AL MVP Award and caught every inning for the Red Sox in a certain World Series. But while it's true that Howard went behind the plate for the Sox in every game of the 1967 fall fray after earlier winning a MVP trophy with the Yankees, he did not catch every inning. Remarkably, he did not even start the 1967 Series opener. What Sox rookie receiver who compiled just 181 career ML hits (the last coming with the 1972 Giants) shocked Cards ace Bob Gibson when he started the opener in Howard's stead? End on a three-run homer.

AB: 15
Hits: 15
Total Bases: 33
RBI: 16

ANSWER SECTION

GAME 1

INNING 1: RED-HOT ROOKIES

1. Babe Ruth.
2. Walt Dropo.
3. Patsy Dougherty.
4. Frank Malzone.
5. Buck O'Brien.
6. Hugh Bedient.
7. Dave Sisler.
8. Don Buddin.
9. Brian Daubach; 1999.
10. Dave "Boo" Ferriss.
11. Ted Cox; 1977.
12. Tom Oliver.
13. Dave Morehead; 1963.
14. Dick Gernert.
15. Smokey Joe Wood.

INNING 2: WHAT WAS THEIR REAL HANDLE?

1. William.
2. Ivan.
3. Myron.
4. Julius.
5. Americo.
6. Nathaniel.
7. Louis.
8. Clell.
9. John.
10. James.
11. Charles.
12. No, not Murrell, which was his middle name—James.
13. Maurice.

14. Elijah.
15. Covelli.

INNING 3: MASTER MOUNDSMEN

1. Pedro Martinez; 2000.
2. Mel Parnell.
3. Joe Wood, with 34 wins in 1912.
4. Mel Parnell; 1949.
5. Wes Ferrell; 1935.
6. Ray Culp, 1968–1970.
7. Lee Stange, in 1967.
8. Babe Ruth, Jesse Tannehill, Ray Collins, Lefty Grove, and Mel Parnell. Too bad if you guessed Dutch Leonard, who missed by one.
9. Bret Saberhagen; 1998.
10. Bill Lee, with 321.
11. Jesse Tannehill.
12. Willard Nixon.
13. Dutch Leonard in 1914 (.180), Luis Tiant with Cleveland in 1968 (.168), and Pedro Martinez in 2000 (.167).
14. How many said Ellis Kinder? It's Ike Delock.

INNING 4: GOLD GLOVE GOLIATHS

1. Frank Malzone; third base.
2. Fred Lynn; 1975.
3. Doug Griffin; 1972.
4. Reggie Smith; 1968.
5. Carl Yastrzemski; 1977; 38.
6. Everett Scott.
7. Jimmy Piersall.
8. Sammy White, 1954–1955.
9. Carlton Fisk; 1972.
10. Lou Criger; 1903.
11. Carl Mays.
12. Rick Burleson.
13. Harry Hooper.
14. Vern Stephens; 1948–1950.

INNING 5: RBI RULERS

1. Jimmy Collins.
2. Carl Everett; 2000.
3. Vern Stephens; 1949; 159 RBI with a .290 BA.

4. Nomar Garciaparra hit .357 with 104 RBI; 1999.
5. Duffy Lewis.
6. Duffy Lewis again, with 109.
7. Babe Ruth; 1919, with 114.
8. Tommy Harper, in 1974.
9. Jackie Jensen.
10. Del Pratt; 1921, with 102.
11. Earl Webb.
12. 1937; Jimmie Foxx (127), Joe Cronin (110), and Pinky Higgins (106).
13. Jason Varitek, in 2006.
14. Tony Conigliaro, who went to the Angels after the 1970 season.

INNING 6: TEAM TEASERS

1. Braves Field, in 1915 and 1916.
2. 1977; Jim Rice who led the AL with 39, George Scott 33, Butch Hobson 30.
3. Because of a local law saying no Sunday games in Boston could be played within 1,000 feet of a church.
4. 1931.
5. 1964.
6. 1937, led by Jimmie Foxx.
7. 1948.
8. The 1987 club, when they went 78–84, after winning the AL flag the year before.
9. They logged a team-record 835 walks in 1949, which was the year of the walk in the AL, as no fewer than 16 pitchers issued at least 100 free passes.
10. 1909, when Tris Speaker burst onto the scene.
11. 1996.
12. 1918, when World War I shortened the schedule.
13. 1933; Roy Johnson, the brother of Indian Bob Johnson.
14. 1912, with 105 wins.

INNING 7: HOME RUN KINGS

1. Buck Freeman.
2. Nick Esasky; 1989.
3. Ike Boone; 1924.
4. Tom Brunansky, in 1992.
5. Jackie Jensen and Ted Williams.
6. Carlton Fisk; 1972 with 22 jacks.

7. Jack Rothrock.
8. It's Nomar.
9. Phil Todt.
10. Wade Boggs; 1985, when he hit .368 with just eight homers.
11. Dick Gernert, in 1957 and 1958.
12. Troy O'Leary, in 1999.
13. No, not Tom Oliver—Doc Cramer, in 1938.
14. John Valentin; 1995, when he hit 27 homers and swiped 20 sacks.

INNING 8: STELLAR STICKWIELDERS

1. Dale Alexander; 1932, who hit a composite .367 after beginning that season in Detroit.
2. Bill Mueller; 2003.
3. Would you believe just once, when Boggs set the club mark with 240 in 1985?
4. Buck Freeman, with 281 in 1903.
5. Reggie Smith, who led with 37 in 1968 and 33 in 1971.
6. Ted Williams; 1941 and 1942.
7. Rick Miller.
8. Jason Varitek; 2003, when he slugged .512.
9. Dick Gernert, with .415.
10. Ted Williams.
11. Pete Runnels; 1960.
12. Jim Rice; 1977–1979.
13. His 344 TB in 1939 made him the first rookie ever to lead the AL.
14. Jimmie Foxx; 1938.
15. Anybody say Babe Ruth? You're right, in 1918.

INNING 9: FALL CLASSICS

1. Bob Ojeda, in 1986.
2. Patsy Dougherty.
3. Juan Beniquez.
4. Chick Stahl.
5. Tom Hughes.
6. Carl Yastrzemski, Reggie Smith, and Rico Petrocelli.
7. Rudy York.
8. Patsy Dougherty.
9. Bernie Carbo, in 1975.
10. Marty Barrett.
11. Joe Dobson.

12. Calvin Schiraldi.
13. Bob Klinger.
14. Pokey Reese.

GAME 2

INNING 1: STELLAR STICKWIELDERS

1. Carl Yastrzemski; 1980, when he posted a .462 SA at age 41. Ted Williams slugged .645 in his coda but missed the PA qualifier by 10.
2. Tris Speaker (329); 1912.
3. Mark Bellhorn; 2004, when he fanned 177 times.
4. Jimmie Foxx (.704); 1938.
5. Rico Petrocelli; 1969.
6. Bobby Doerr; 1944.
7. Babe Ruth (1.114); 1919.
8. Don Buddin, with a .244 Sox BA.
9. Bill Buckner; 1985.
10. Jimmie Foxx; 1938.
11. John Olerud; 2005.
12. Nomar Garciaparra hit 27 homers with a .603 SA; 1999.
13. Johnny Pesky; 1947.
14. He set a new ML record (since broken) with 53 doubles.

INNING 2: MASTER MOUNDSMEN

1. Joe Wood was 34–5 in 1912 for a .872 winning percentage, the highest by a 30-game winner until Lefty Grove broke it in 1931.
2. Roger Moret, who went 41–18 in Sox garb from 1970–1975.
3. Babe Ruth, with .659 (89–46).
4. Ferguson Jenkins, 1976–1977.
5. Dutch Leonard; 0.96 in 1914, the post-1900 record for the lowest season ERA.
6. Lefty Grove; four.
7. Mickey McDermott.
8. Oscar Judd.
9. David Wells; 2005.
10. Curt Schilling; 2004.
11. Lefty Grove and Mel Parnell.
12. Rick Wise, in 1975.
13. Wes Ferrell; 322⅓ in 1935 and 301 in 1936.

INNING 3: CY YOUNG SIZZLERS

1. Cy Young again, with a league-leading 32 triumphs.
2. Jim Lonborg, in 1967.
3. Jesse Tannehill.
4. Derek Lowe; 2002.
5. Boo Ferriss.
6. Tom Brewer, 19 in 1956 and 16 in 1957.
7. Tex Hughson.
8. Lefty Grove.
9. Walter Johnson.
10. Luis Tiant, in 1972, 1974, and 1976.
11. Jack Kramer.
12. Pedro Martinez, earned his first Cy Young with the 1999 Sox after winning 10 relief games with the 1993 Dodgers.
13. Joe Dobson.
14. Tim Wakefield; 1995.

INNING 4: BULLPEN BLAZERS

1. Ellis Kinder.
2. Bob Stanley; 1982.
3. Dick Radatz; 1964; 181.
4. Heathcliff Slocumb.
5. Bill Henry.
6. Bob Klinger.
7. Ted Lewis.
8. Wilcy Moore; 1931, with 10 saves and 15 starts.
9. Jim Willoughby.
10. Joe Heving.
11. Jeff Reardon.
12. Uggie Urbina, saved 40 in 2002 and went to the slammer in 2007.
13. Mark Clear; 1982.

INNING 5: WHO'D THEY COME UP WITH

1. Washington AA; 1891.
2. Florida Marlins; 1998.
3. Brooklyn NL; 1893.
4. Cleveland; 1958.
5. Cleveland; 1939.
6. Washington NL; 1898.
7. Nope, not Washington—none other than the BoSox; 1940.

8. Philadelphia A's; 1937.
9. Kansas City; 1995.
10. Washington; 1951.
11. Pittsburgh Pirates; 1976.
12. Chicago White Sox; 1941.
13. St. Louis Browns; 1946.
14. Los Angeles Dodgers; 1992.
15. Cincinnati Reds; 1908.

INNING 6: FAMOUS FEATS

1. Bill Mueller, on July 29, 2003.
2. Jim Lonborg, in 1967.
3. Jim Tabor and Ted Williams, in 1939.
4. Carlton Fisk; he played for Dick Williams, Eddie Popowski, and then Eddie Kasko.
5. Ted Williams; 1946, when Mickey Vernon led.
6. Babe Ruth; 1916 at age 21 years, 65 days.
7. Orlando Cepeda; 1973.
8. Jimmie Foxx, Joe Cronin, Jim Tabor, and Ted Williams.
9. Joe Cronin; 1943.
10. He cracked three hits in the inning. BoSoxer Johnny Damon is the only ALer who has done it since.
11. Jimmy Piersall.
12. Howard Ehmke, in 1923.
13. Sonny Siebert, in 1971.
14. Willard Nixon.

INNING 7: MEMORABLE MONIKERS

1. Tris Speaker.
2. Carlton Fisk.
3. Eric McNair.
4. Dick Radatz.
5. Paul Trout.
6. Dave Ferriss.
7. Don Zimmer.
8. Clarence Walker.
9. Chester Thomas.
10. George Scott and David Wells.
11. Lamar Newsome.
12. Rich Garces.
13. Bob Smith.

14. Steve Lyons.
15. Harry Agganis.

INNING 8: FORGOTTEN UNFORGETTABLES

1. Lou Clinton.
2. Jerry Moses.
3. Johnny Lazor.
4. Joe Hesketh.
5. Olaf Henriksen.
6. Scott Cooper, the BoSox' only All-Star in 1993 and 1994.
7. Charlie Armbruster.
8. Gene Stephens; Vern Stephens.
9. Jack Wilson.
10. Jack Russell; Washington.
11. Ike Boone.
12. John Curtis.
13. Willie Tasby, in 1960.
14. Dwayne Hosey, 1995–1996.

INNING 9: RBI RULERS

1. Ken Harrelson, with 109 RBI in 1968.
2. Jimmie Foxx; 175 RBI in 1938.
3. Bill Buckner in 1986 posted 102 RBI and fanned 25 times.
4. Vern Stephens.
5. Ted Williams (123), Rudy York (119), and Bobby Doerr (116).
6. Reggie Smith drove in 96; 1971.
7. 1952; Dick Gernert.
8. Earl Webb; 1931.
9. Frank Malzone; 1957.
10. Tom Brunansky; 1992, with 74 RBI.
11. Vic Wertz.
12. Buck Freeman (1902–1903), Jackie Jensen (1958–1959), and David Ortiz (2005–2006).
13. Sammy White, with 404.
14. Mo Vaughn and Albert Belle both posted 126; 1995.

GAME 3

INNING 1: SHELL-SHOCKED SLINGERS

1. Lefty Grove; 1934, when he posted a 6.50 ERA.
2. Jack Lamabe.

3. Red Ruffing.
4. Steve Avery; 1998.
5. Joe Harris; in 1906 he was 2–21.
6. Don Schwall.
7. Red Ruffing again; 1928 and 1929.
8. Ramon Martinez; 2000.
9. 1906; Cy Young, George Winter, Bill Dinneen, and Joe Harris.
10. 1930; Milt Gaston and Jack Russell.
11. Bill Lee; 1974, when he yielded 320 hits.
12. Hal Wiltse.
13. Eddie Cicotte.
14. Tom Brewer.
15. Mel Parnell; 1955.

INNING 2: HOME RUN KINGS

1. Carl Yastrzemski; 22.
2. Frank Malzone, with 133 dingers.
3. Rico Petrocelli, with 40 homers and 97 RBI; 1969; shortstop.
4. Hugh Bradley.
5. Tilly Walker, in 1918.
6. David Ortiz, cracked 43 as a DH in 2005 and 47 from that slot in 2006.
7. Jim Tabor, who hit 90.
8. Otis Nixon; 1994.
9. Dom DiMaggio.
10. Yep, Dom DiMaggio again.
11. Bob Tillman.
12. Carl Yastrzemski.
13. Del Gainer, Joe Wood, Jake Stahl, Babe Ruth, and Buck Freeman. How many got both Wood and Gainer?
14. Mo Vaughn, 1993–1998.

INNING 3: MASTER MOUNDSMEN

1. Herb Pennock.
2. Howard Ehmke and Danny MacFayden.
3. Jack Quinn.
4. Joe Bush, in 1918.
5. Mel Parnell and Bob Stanley.
6. Danny Darwin, in 1993.
7. Carl Mays (21), Sam Jones (16), Joe Bush (15), Babe Ruth (13).

8. Cy Young, Bill Dinneen, and Long Tom Hughes; Norwood Gibson was the 13-game winner.

9. Frank Sullivan; 1955.

10. Mel Parnell; 21 in 1953.

11. Howard Ehmke; 20–17 in 1923.

12. Joe Wood; 1910.

13. Tex Hughson.

INNING 4: NO-HIT NUGGETS

1. 1904; Cy Young; Rube Waddell.

2. Rube Foster; Dutch Leonard; 1916.

3. Earl Wilson; 1962.

4. Cy Young; 1904 and 1908.

5. Ernie Shore; he replaced Babe Ruth on June 23, 1917, after Ruth was booted for arguing a ball call that resulted in a walk to Washington leadoff hitter Ray Morgan, and Morgan was cut down trying to steal shortly after Shore entered the game.

6. Matt Young; 1992.

7. Howard Ehmke; Philadelphia.

8. It had been 33 years since Howard Ehmke's no-no in 1923.

9. Bill Carrigan, caught one in 1911 and two more in 1916.

10. Joe Wood was just 21 when he did it in 1911.

11. Derek Lowe; 2002.

12. Dave Morehead; Luis Tiant.

13. Hideo Nomo; 2001.

14. Bill Monbouquette; 1962; catcher Jim Pagliaroni.

15. Clay Buchholz, in 2007.

INNING 5: WHAT WAS THEIR REAL HANDLE?

1. Christopher.

2. Preston.

3. Anthony.

4. Cecil.

5. Truman.

6. George.

7. Spike, what else?

8. George.

9. Carl.

10. David (and his middle name is Jonathan, making his real initials the reverse of his baseball ones).

11. Dennis.

12. Garland.
13. Albert.
14. Robert.
15. Howard.

INNING 6: CIRCLING THE GLOBE

1. Juan Marichal; 1974.
2. Ted Lewis.
3. Vicente Romo.
4. Bunk Congalton.
5. Mike Fornieles.
6. Mike Herrera.
7. Tony Welzer.
8. Bobby Thomson.
9. Oscar Judd.
10. Win Remmerswaal.
11. Tomo Ohka; 1999.
12. Tony Pena.
13. Mel Almada.
14. Reggie Cleveland, lost Game 5 in 1975.

INNING 7: STELLAR STICKWIELDERS

1. Chick Stahl; committed suicide during spring training in 1907 after his team-best 1906 campaign.
2. Earl Webb; 67; 1931.
3. Joe Cronin, in 1938.
4. Jimmy Piersall; 1956.
5. Nomar Garciaparra, with 51 in 2000 and 56 in 2002.
6. Reggie Jefferson, in 1996 and 1997.
7. Chick Stahl and Buck Freeman; 1904.
8. Tris Speaker; 1913.
9. It's been 46 years since Chick Stahl and Buck Freeman tied with Washington's Joe Cassidy for the AL lead in 1904.
10. Pete Runnels; 1957.
11. Luis Aparicio; 1973.
12. Bing Miller.
13. Long Tom Hughes finished at .301.
14. David Ortiz batted .287 with a ML-leading 1.049 OPS in 2006.
15. Fred Lynn; 1979.

INNING 8: RBI RULERS

1. Doc Cramer.
2. Jim Tabor, who plated over 500.
3. Tony Armas; 1983; .218.
4. Shame on you if you said Ruth—it was Wes Ferrell.
5. Dick Gernert.
6. Hope you steered clear of Nomar, because it's John Valentin with 102 in 1995.
7. Stuffy McInnis.
8. Norm Zauchin, with 27 homers and 93 RBI in 1955.
9. Butch Hobson drove in 112 in 1977.
10. Tim Hendryx.
11. 1975, when rookies Fred Lynn and Jim Rice finished 1–2 on the club in RBI with 105 and 102, respectively; Rick Burleson.
12. Dick Stuart led the Sox in his only two years in Boston.
13. Roy and Bob Johnson.
14. Rick Ferrell, in 1935.

INNING 9: RED-HOT ROOKIES

1. Home runs.
2. George Stone.
3. Billy Consolo.
4. Ike Boone, with .337 in 1924.
5. Doug Griffin.
6. Joe Harris; 2.
7. John Curtis, in 1972.
8. George Winter.
9. Jim Lonborg; 1965.
10. Amby McConnell.
11. Harry Lord.
12. Tris Speaker; 1909.
13. Dick Newsome—the infielder was Skeeter Newsome.
14. Freddy Parent, who debuted with St. Louis in 1899.
15. Eddie Pellagrini, with 71 at bats.

GAME 4

INNING 1: JACK OF ALL TRADES

1. Pete Runnels.
2. Steve Lyons.
3. Jack Rothrock; 1928.

4. First base.
5. First base, second base, third base, left field, right field.
6. John Valentin.
7. Ron Mahay.
8. Buck Freeman.
9. Jerry Adair, in 1967.
10. Eric McNair.
11. Third base; 1928.
12. Ed Romero.
13. Hal Janvrin.
14. Bobby Doerr, with 1,852 games at second base. Note that Ted Williams played left field and right field and also pitched one game.

INNING 2: HOME RUN KINGS

1. Cy Young.
2. Billy Goodman.
3. Ken Harrelson.
4. Harry Hooper.
5. Everett Scott.
6. Trot Nixon, hit 133 taters for Boston.
7. Ted Lepcio, with 3.13 per 100 AB.
8. Ted Williams, Jimmie Foxx, Jackie Jensen, Vern Stephens, and the tough one, Dick Gernert.
9. Clyde Vollmer.
10. Rich Gedman cracked 22 as a catcher, plus two more as a pinch stick in 1986.
11. Ted Williams; 1953, with 13 home runs in just 91 AB.
12. Tris Speaker, in 1915.
13. Eddie Lake.

INNING 3: TUMULTUOUS TRADES

1. Hanley Ramirez and Anibal Sanchez went to Florida. Josh Beckett and Mike Lowell were the key figures acquired.
2. Patsy Dougherty.
3. Freddy Sanchez, in a deal with Pittsburgh in 2003.
4. Jesse Burkett was traded to the St. Louis Browns for George Stone.
5. Ben Oglivie.
6. Tris Speaker.
7. Clyde Vollmer.
8. Vic Wertz and Gary Geiger.
9. Herb Pennock.

10. Harry Hooper.
11. Dennis Eckersley, in 1978.
12. Dale Alexander.
13. Johnny Marcum.
14. Larry Andersen and Jeff Bagwell.

INNING 4: TEAM TEASERS

1. 2003; Grady Little.
2. 1968, when the Sox hit .236 and Yaz led the AL at .301.
3. 1927, while Babe Ruth was hitting 60 all by himself.
4. 1950, when the Sox hit .302.
5. Carl Yastrzemski, Carlton Fisk, Dwight Evans, and Rick Burleson.
6. 1906.
7. 1973–1974.
8. 1944.
9. 1965.
10. Lefty Grove, Joe Cronin, Rick Ferrell, Jimmie Foxx, and the toughie, Heinie Manush.
11. 1992.
12. 1925.
13. 1963, when the strike zone was expanded to encompass the tops of the shoulders to the bottom of the knees.
14. 2002; Pedro Martinez and Derek Lowe.

INNING 5: MVP MARVELS

1. Tris Speaker.
2. Del Pratt.
3. Ira Flagstead.
4. Buddy Myer.
5. Earl Webb.
6. 1985, when he placed a distant fourth.
7. Carl Yastrzemski; 1967.
8. Wes Ferrell.
9. Jimmie Foxx; 1938.
10. Twice; 1941 and 1942.
11. Tony Armas; 1984; born in Venezuela.
12. Billy Goodman.
13. Tony Conigliaro at age 20; 1965.
14. Ted Williams and Vic Wertz.
15. Rick Miller.

INNING 6: MOMENTS TO REMEMBER

1. Manny Ramirez, J. D. Drew, Mike Lowell, and Jason Varitek.
2. Mike Greenwell, in 1996.
3. Earl Johnson.
4. Bill Lefebvre; 1938.
5. Steve Yerkes.
6. Johnny Pesky, in 1946, and Spike Owen, in 1986.
7. Dave Shean.
8. Tommy Dowd, who debuted with Boston's American Association flag winner in 1891.
9. Rudy York.
10. Everett Scott.
11. Pinky Higgins.
12. Billy Rohr; Russ Gibson.
13. Mike Ryba.
14. Don Gile.

INNING 7: PEERLESS PILOTS

1. Bill Carrigan.
2. Including nineteenth-century World Series and Temple Cup play, Collins was the first postseason player-manager who was a third baseman.
3. Dick Williams, in 1967.
4. Jack Barry; 1917.
5. Ed Barrow; Yankees club president/GM.
6. Joe Morgan; 1988.
7. Chick Stahl.
8. George Huff.
9. Billy Herman; 1965; the Kansas City A's.
10. 1908; Deacon McGuire and Fred Lake.
11. Patsy Donovan; 1912.
12. Hugh Duffy, 1921–1922.
13. Bill Carrigan.
14. Pete Runnels; served as interim skipper at the close of the 1966 season.
15. Frank Chance; 1913 Yankees and 1923 Red Sox.

INNING 8: RED-HOT ROOKIES

1. Jake Jones, in 1947.
2. Billy Goodman; 1948.
3. Everett Scott.

4. Sam Mele; 1947.
5. Babe Dahlgren, replaced Lou Gehrig.
6. Johnny Pesky, as a shortstop in 1942.
7. Rabbit Warstler.
8. Dom DiMaggio; 1940.
9. Phil Todt.
10. Tom Umphlett.
11. Ike Boone, with 13 in 1924.
12. Jim Tabor.
13. Jerry Casale.
14. Norm Zauchin.
15. Harry Agganis, who died tragically of pneumonia early in his sophomore ML season.

INNING 9: FALL CLASSICS

1. Bill Mueller.
2. Olaf Henriksen.
3. Denny Galehouse, who did not join the team until 1947.
4. Norm Siebern.
5. Roy Partee and Hal Wagner.
6. Larry Gardner.
7. Fred Thomas.
8. Chick Stahl, with 10 in 1903.
9. Ernie Shore.
10. Jake Stahl, Steve Yerkes, Heinie Wagner, and Larry Gardner.
11. How many of you said Cy Young or Bill Dinneen in 1903? It was Buck O'Brien in 1912.
12. Bill Carrigan; Hick Cady.
13. Jose Santiago.
14. Joe Bush.

GAME 5

INNING 1: ALL IN THE FAMILY

1. Pedro and Ramon Martinez, 1999–2000.
2. Lou and Hal Finney.
3. Tony and Billy Conigliaro; 1970.
4. Jim Delahanty.
5. Milt and Alex Gaston.
6. Wes and Rick Ferrell.

7. George and Dave Sisler.
8. Bill and Ray Narleski.
9. Shano Collins and his grandson Bob Gallagher.
10. John and Joe Heving.
11. Haywood and Marc Sullivan.
12. Glenn and Trevor Hoffman.
13. Brian and Denny Doyle.
14. Marty and Tom Barrett, Spike and Dave Owen.

INNING 2: RBI RULERS

1. Pinky Higgins, in 1937 and 1938.
2. Bill Buckner; 1985–1986.
3. Bobby Doerr; 1950.
4. None other than Pinky Higgins again, in 1937 and 1938.
5. Nomar Garciaparra; 1997–1999.
6. Tony Perez, in 1980.
7. Frank Malzone; 1961–1962.
8. Johnny Peacock.
9. Tony Armas; 1984.
10. Clyde Vollmer.
11. Fred Lynn; 1975.
12. Vic Wertz; 1960.
13. Mike Greenwell, in 1988.
14. Joe Cronin, with 29 RBI in 77 AB in 1943.

INNING 3: CY YOUNG SIZZLERS

1. Howard Ehmke.
2. Rick Wise.
3. Mel Parnell; 1949.
4. Lefty Grove.
5. Curt Schilling, in 2004.
6. Carl Mays.
7. Bill Campbell; 1977.
8. Ernie Shore.
9. Bruce Hurst; 1988.
10. Bill Lee, with 94.
11. Bill Monbouquette won 20 in 1963.
12. Roger Clemens; 1986.
13. Dennis Eckersley, 1978–1979 with the Sox, and later won it with the 1992 A's.
14. Bob Stanley, in 1978 and 1982.

INNING 4: ODD COMBO ACHIEVEMENTS

1. Jim Rice, stroked 15 to lead the AL in 1977, plus 15 more in 1978.
2. Frank Sullivan, lost 16 in 153⅔ innings in 1960.
3. Ed Connolly.
4. Duffy Lewis, in 1913.
5. Bob Stanley, who went 15–2 in 1978 and 4–15 in 1987.
6. Games played, which was held at the time by Harry Hooper.
7. False. Ruth led in home runs with Buck Freeman second, but Dutch Leonard led in lefty wins with Ruth second.
8. Home run percentage, which belonged at the time to Jimmie Foxx.
9. Wally Schang.
10. Stuffy McInnis.
11. Danny MacFayden.
12. Jackie Jensen, who went tripleless in 1958 and 1959.
13. Harry Hooper, who hit .235 in 1915 and .242 in 1912.
14. Stuffy McInnis and Rabbit Warstler.

INNING 5: BRAZEN BASE THIEVES

1. Buddy Myer; 1928.
2. Jackie Jensen; 1954.
3. Billy Werber, 1934–1935.
4. Dom DiMaggio; 1950; stole 15 bases.
5. Harry Hooper; 1910.
6. Duffy Lewis.
7. Tommy Harper; 1973.
8. Tris Speaker; 1912.
9. Harry Hooper; 300.
10. Walt Dropo.
11. Johnny Damon.
12. Otis Nixon.
13. Joe Foy stole 26 bases at third; 1968.
14. Carl Yastrzemski, with 23 in 1970.

INNING 6: HOME RUN KINGS

1. Hobe Ferris, with 34.
2. Mark Bellhorn; 2004; second base.
3. Jerry Remy, in 1982 and 1983.
4. Billy Werber; 14 in 1935.
5. Gary Geiger.

6. Dick Stuart, in 1963.
7. Vern Stephens.
8. Reggie Smith, who belted 149 homers with the Sox, 1966–1973.
9. Deron Johnson and Rico Petrocelli.
10. Felix Mantilla; 1964.
11. Rick Ferrell.
12. Ellis Burks; 1990.
13. Norm Zauchin; hit 27 in 1955 with a .239 BA.

INNING 7: RED-HOT ROOKIES

1. Jonathan Papelbon; 2006.
2. Sammy White, with 10 in 1952.
3. Denny Sullivan.
4. Mike Andrews, in 1967.
5. Freddy Parent.
6. Billy Klaus. His brother was Bobby.
7. Sam Horn; 1987.
8. Ken Brett, in 1970.
9. Ellis Burks; 1987.
10. Joe Foy; 1966.
11. George Scott; he teamed with Joe Foy in 1966.
12. Russ Scarritt.
13. Mike Nagy; 1969.
14. Ted Wingfield.
15. Al Nipper; 1984.

INNING 8: THE NAME'S THE SAME

1. Darren, Duffy, and Ted Lewis.
2. Otis, Trot, and Willard Nixon.
3. Earl, Roy, and Bob Johnson.
4. Pinch, George, and Tommy Thomas.
5. Joe Harris.
6. Hal, Heinie, and Charlie Wagner.
7. Hack, Otto, and Rick Miller.
8. Haywood, Denny, and Frank Sullivan.
9. Marty, Frank, and Jimmy Barrett.
10. Allan, Jack, and Jeff Russell.
11. Ed, Cy, and Joe Morgan.
12. Tilly, Chico, and Todd Walker.
13. Jack, Jim, and Earl Wilson.
14. Ray, Shano, and Jimmy Collins.

INNING 9: MASTER MOUNDSMEN

1. Pedro Martinez, in 2002.
2. Aaron Sele; 1995.
3. Bob Ojeda; 1984.
4. Hugh Bedient, in 1912.
5. 1917; 24.
6. Roger Clemens; 1986 (.195).
7. Jack Chesbro; 1909.
8. Dick Ellsworth, in 1968.
9. Sonny Siebert.
10. Mel Parnell, with 123.
11. Luis Tiant; 1974.
12. Bill Lee, 1973–1975.
13. David Wells; 2005.
14. Bill Monboquette, 1962–1965.

GAME 6

INNING 1: HOME RUN KINGS

1. Gavy Cravath, as a member of the Phils led the NL in dingers six times; Babe Ruth also led the AL six times in seven seasons at one point, but his last homer crown came at age 36.
2. Tony Conigliaro.
3. Dwight Evans; nine seasons, 1981–1989.
4. Buck Freeman, who cracked an NL-leading 25 homers with Washington in 1899.
5. Orlando Cepeda, the Sox' first DH in 1973.
6. Ted Williams and Bobby Doerr.
7. Carl Yastrzemski; 1969.
8. Tilly Walker.
9. Jimmie Foxx belted 35 at Fenway in 1938.
10. Butch Hobson; 1977.
11. Mike Stanley; 1996.
12. Del Wilber.
13. Jose Canseco, in 1995 and 1996.
14. Vern Stephens, with 4.79.

INNING 2: STELLAR STICKWIELDERS

1. Johnny Pesky.
2. Rick Ferrell, at .302.

3. Buddy Myer.
4. Ted Williams; 1949.
5. Patsy Dougherty.
6. Lou Criger, with .208.
7. Carl Yastrzemski in 1970 and Wade Boggs in 1988.
8. Freddy Parent.
9. Doc Cramer (.727), Lou Finney (.762), Buddy Myer (.762), Billy Goodman (.773), Patsy Dougherty (.783), Joe Vosmik (.790), and Johnny Pesky (.794).
10. Dusty Cooke.
11. Jimmie Foxx, Vern Stephens, and Bobby Doerr.
12. Jimmie Foxx (.320), Pete Runnels (.319), George Burns (.317).
13. Wade Boggs; 1986–1989.
14. Not Teddy Ballgame, it's Bobby Doerr with 238 hits in 1936.
15. Freddy Parent.

INNING 3: MEMORABLE MONIKERS

1. Ken Harrelson.
2. Rick Burleson.
3. Walter Evers.
4. Bill Lee.
5. George Tebbetts.
6. Ralph Houk.
7. Harold Warstler.
8. Alfred Walters.
9. Dick Stuart.
10. Dom DiMaggio.
11. George Cuppy.
12. Roger Clemens.
13. Forrest Cady.
14. David Ortiz.
15. Charles Hall.

INNING 4: BULLPEN BLAZERS

1. Tom Burgmeier, in 1980.
2. Lee Smith.
3. John Wyatt.
4. Rick Aguilera, in 1995.
5. Frank Arellanes.
6. Keith Foulke; 2004.
7. Tom Gordon; 1998–1999.

8. Carl Mays.
9. Dick Drago.
10. Charley Hall.
11. Jack Wilson.
12. Mike Timlin, who made an AL-leading 81 appearances in 2005.
13. Jimmie Foxx and Ted Williams; 1939 and 1940, respectively.
14. Earl Johnson.

INNING 5: GOLD GLOVE GOLIATHS

1. Mike Boddicker; 1990.
2. Billy Goodman.
3. Hope you didn't say Jason Varitek, because it was Tony Pena; 1991.
4. Joe Dobson.
5. Jimmie Foxx.
6. Dwight Evans.
7. Frank Malzone, 1957–1959; Brooks Robinson.
8. Jason Varitek; 2005.
9. Mark Loretta; 2006.
10. Dom DiMaggio; 1948.
11. Ellis Burks; 1990.
12. Grady Hatton, in 1955; Mike Lowell, who fielded .987 in 2006.
13. George Scott; first and third, with Gold Gloves coming at the gateway spot in 1967, 1968, and 1971.
14. Vern Stephens.

INNING 6: SHELL-SHOCKED SLINGERS

1. Dennis Eckersley, in 1983.
2. Cy Young.
3. Frank Sullivan.
4. Tom Gordon; 1996.
5. Red Ruffing 5.01 and Paul Zahniser 5.15.
6. Luis Tiant; 1973.
7. Ted Lewis.
8. Bob Porterfield.
9. Buster Ross.
10. Tim Wakefield.
11. Earl Wilson.
12. Josh Beckett; 2006.

13. Sam Jones, in 1919.
14. Bill Monboquette and Dave Morehead; 1965.

INNING 7: HEROES AND GOATS

1. Bill Buckner.
2. George Whiteman.
3. Edgar Renteria.
4. Leon Culberson.
5. Butch Hobson; 1978.
6. Joe Wood; 1912.
7. Harry Hooper; 1915.
8. Denny Galehouse.
9. Ted Williams.
10. Candy LaChance.
11. Bruce Hurst, in 1986.
12. Jim Burton.
13. Cecil Cooper.

INNING 8: RED-HOT ROOKIES

1. Nomar Garciaparra; 1997.
2. Ed Morris.
3. Wade Boggs, in 1982.
4. Hobe Ferris.
5. Carlton Fisk; 1972.
6. Jody Reed; 1988.
7. Don Schwall, in 1961.
8. Bill Henry.
9. Gleason; Harry, brother of Kid.
10. Fred Lynn; 1975.
11. Jim Bagby Jr.
12. Carlos Quintana; 1990.
13. Jim Rice; 1975.
14. Reggie Smith and Rod Carew; 1967.

INNING 9: PEERLESS PILOTS

1. Joe McCarthy; in 1948 and again in 1949.
2. Lou Boudreau, 1952–1954; 1948 Indians.
3. Darrell Johnson, who played with the 1957–1958 Yanks.
4. Pinky Higgins, in 1960.
5. Terry Francona.
6. John McNamara, in 1986. Ed Barrow, who also never played in the majors, is in Cooperstown.

7. Ralph Houk, in 1984.

8. Lee Fohl, 1924–1926. For shame if you bit and guessed Bill Carrigan.

9. Hope you didn't say Grady Little, because it's Don Zimmer with 99; 1978.

10. Eddie Kasko, in 1970–1973.

11. Steve O'Neill; managed the 1945 Tigers and played for the 1920 World Champion Indians.

12. Fred Lake.

13. Joe Kerrigan; 2001.

14. Lou Boudreau, in 1953 and 1954.

GAME 7

INNING 1: RBI RULERS

1. Jack Clark; 1991.
2. Vern Stephens and Bobby Doerr; 1948–1950.
3. Jackie Gutierrez; 1984.
4. Jim Tabor, with 81.
5. David Ortiz had 144 RBI; Manny Ramirez plated 148; 2005.
6. Bobby Veach.
7. Frank Malzone; 1957.
8. George Burns.
9. George Kell; 1953.
10. Tris Speaker; 1909 with 77.
11. Manny Ramirez, in 2002.
12. Earl Webb.
13. Doc Gessler.
14. Bill "Rough" Carrigan.

INNING 2: MVP MARVELS

1. Fred Lynn; 1975.
2. 1946.
3. Mel Parnell and Ellis Kinder; 1949.
4. 1947; Joe DiMaggio.
5. Ken Harrelson, in 1968.
6. Dick Radatz, in 1963.
7. David Ortiz, 2003–2006.
8. Dwight Evans, who played 2,505 games in Sox garb.
9. Jackie Jensen; 1958.

10. Jim Rice; 1978.
11. Carl Yastrzemski; 1967.
12. Mo Vaughn; 1995.
13. Roger Clemens; 1986.
14. Mike Fornieles; 1960.

INNING 3: TUMULTUOUS TRADES

1. The Sox surrendered Sparky Lyle for Danny Cater.
2. Lefty Grove, Rube Walberg, and Max Bishop, in 1933.
3. Wes Ferrell.
4. Derek Lowe and Jason Varitek.
5. Joe Cronin.
6. Cecil Cooper.
7. Curt Schilling and Brady Anderson.
8. Tony Armas Jr. and Carl Pavano.
9. George Pipgras.
10. Carl Mays.
11. Vern Stephens and Jack Kramer.
12. Waite Hoyt and Wally Schang, in 1920.
13. Buddy Myer.
14. Jackie Jensen, in 1953.

INNING 4: WHO'D THEY COME UP WITH?

1. New York Yankees; 1950.
2. San Francisco; 1997.
3. Boston NL; 1895.
4. Minnesota Twins; 1997.
5. Milwaukee Brewers; 1993.
6. Cleveland NL; 1896.
7. Philadelphia A's; 1912.
8. Pittsburgh Pirates; 1992.
9. New York Giants; 1912.
10. Minnesota Twins; 1973.
11. New York Giants; 1902.
12. Minnesota Twins; 1990.
13. San Francisco; 1996.
14. New York NL; 1890.
15. St. Louis Cardinals; 1967.

INNING 5: STRIKEOUT KINGS

1. Tex Hughson tied for the lead in 1942 with 113.
2. Joe Wood; 1911 with 231.

3. Roger Clemens; 1988.
4. Joe Dobson, with 116.
5. Hideo Nomo, in 2001.
6. Lefty Grove; 1937.
7. Pedro Martinez, 1999–2000.
8. Slim Harriss; Red Ruffing.
9. Jim Lonborg, with 246; 1967.
10. Ike Delock.
11. Cy Young, with 1,341.
12. Dutch Leonard; 1914.
13. Bruce Hurst, fanned 190 in 1987 and 189 in 1985.
14. Dick Radatz; fanned a relief-record 181 batters in 1964.

INNING 6: STELLAR STICKWIELDERS

1. Ed Bressoud, whose .293 BA topped Sox regulars in 1964.
2. Babe Ruth, on May 19, 1918. His five hits included three doubles and a triple.
3. Wade Boggs, 1985–1991.
4. Carl Yastrzemski; 1963.
5. Jim Rice had 406 in 1978; Joe Dimaggio amassed 418 with the Yankees in 1937.
6. Johnny Damon, 2002–2005.
7. Glenn Hoffman, who hit .209 in 1982.
8. It's the Sox all-time hit leader, Carl Yastrzemski, with 2,262 singles.
9. Trot Nixon; 2003.
10. Frank Malzone.
11. Tom Brunansky, in 1992.
12. Bob Johnson; .959 OPS in 1944.
13. Mike Greenwell, 1985–1996.
14. Nomar Garciaparra hit 27 homers with a .603 SA; 1999.

INNING 7: HOME RUN KINGS

1. Lee Thomas.
2. 1918.
3. Tony Armas; 1984.
4. Dwight Evans; 1981; hit 22 homers, tying with Tony Armas, Bobby Grich, and Eddie Murray.
5. Buck Freeman; 1901–1903.
6. Babe Ruth; 1919.
7. Hobe Ferris.

8. Jim Pagliaroni; caught Catfish Hunter's perfecto for the A's in 1968.

9. Jim Rice; 1977.

10. Tony Conigliaro had exactly 20 homers in 1967 when he was beaned to bring an abrupt end to his season with just 389 PA.

11. Candy LaChance.

12. Smead Jolley.

13. Jake Stahl; 1910.

14. Harry Hooper.

INNING 8: MASTER MOUNDSMEN

1. Dennis Eckersley, in 1978 and 1998.
2. Tom Seaver, in 1986.
3. Pedro Martinez, in 1999, and Curt Schilling, in 2004.
4. Greg Harris; 1991.
5. Luis Tiant; 1974.
6. Babe Ruth, who worked 323⅔ homerless innings in 1916.
7. Tim Wakefield, who won 17 during a season in which he turned 41; 2007.
8. Oil Can Boyd.
9. Dennis Eckersley, 1978–1979.
10. Jesse Tannehill.
11. Jose Santiago.
12. Bill Dinneen; 1902.
13. Sam Jones.
14. Jim Lonborg, in 1967.
15. Josh Beckett, who won 20 in 2007.

INNING 9: FALL CLASSICS

1. Patsy Dougherty; replaced by Kip Selbach.
2. Dave Shean.
3. Tim Blackwell.
4. Rico Petrocelli.
5. Don Baylor, in 1986.
6. John Wyatt, in Game 6.
7. 1918.
8. Ken Brett.
9. Steve Crawford.
10. Dwight Evans. Jim Rice was injured and missed the 1975 postseason.
11. Luis Tiant shut out the Reds 6–0 in the 1975 Series opener.

12. Gary Waslewski, in 1967.
13. Al Nipper, in 1986.
14. Babe Ruth, in 1918, Game 4; Sam Agnew.
15. Russ Gibson, who faced his namesake Bob in his first World Series at bat.

ABOUT THE AUTHORS

David Nemec is among the best-selling baseball writers in the United States. His *Great Baseball Feats, Facts and Firsts* has sold over 700,000 copies in various editions, the most recent of which was coauthored with **Scott Flatow**. Between them, Nemec and Flatow have won ten National Trivia Contests sponsored by the Society for American Baseball Research.